WC

WALKING *with* WORDSWORTH
in the Lake District

Norman & June Buckley

F
FRANCES LINCOLN LIMITED
PUBLISHERS

Frances Lincoln Limited
4 Torriano Mews
Torriano Avenue
London NW5 2RZ
www.franceslincoln.com

PAGES 2—3 Latrigg, near Keswick

CONTENTS

Location plan 6
Introduction 7

WALKS

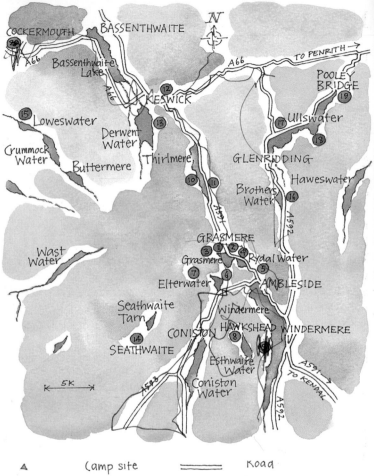

▲	Camp site	═══ Road
■	Building	------- Walk
Ⓟ	Car park	→ Direction
⊖	Bus station	Ⓢ Start of walk
+	Church	① Walk reference points
- - - - - -	Footpath	Lake, stream, river
══════	Track	.... Ferry

INTRODUCTION

First and foremost, this is a book of walks, not an attempt to apply scholarship to any facet of the life or works of the great poet William Wordsworth. Each walk is described with introductory information concerning length, amount of ascent, car parking and refreshments, and the relevant map. There is also an outline of the nature of the walk and any noteworthy features. The route is then set out in detail, accompanied by a sketch plan. The walks are predominantly short and relatively easy, although there are just a few longer and more difficult routes.

The distinction from other walking books, though, is that each route has a clear association with Wordsworth, that association being set out in the accompanying text. Throughout his long life, Wordsworth was an avid walker, taking on the one hand short local walks at virtually any time of day (or night!), pacing up and down a favourite path, seeking inspiration, and on the other hand much longer walks, such as his tour of the Lakes as a young man in 1799 with his friend the poet Samuel Taylor Coleridge.

After spending his early childhood (1770 to 1779) at Cockermouth and his school years (1779 to 1787) at Hawkshead, he returned to the Lake District in 1799 when, with his sister Dorothy, he became the tenant of Dove Cottage, Grasmere. As his family grew — he married Mary Hutchinson in 1802 — he needed more living space, and he resided from 1808 to 1811 at Allan Bank and from 1811 to 1813 at The Rectory, both in Grasmere. His final move was to nearby Rydal Mount in 1813, where he remained until his death in 1850. From Grasmere he walked to and

Wordsworth in old age

Dorothy Wordsworth

from Greta Lodge, Keswick, the home of Coleridge and the poet Robert Southey, and to and from Eusemere, near Pooley Bridge, the home of his friends Thomas and Catherine Clarkson, comparatively frequently. He also occasionally climbed mountains, then a daring undertaking, for many necessitating the employment of a guide. It is recorded that he climbed Scafell Pike, Skiddaw, Helvellyn and Seat Sandal. His walking was by no means confined to the Lake District — in his youthful years he walked around the West Country and extensively in France and Italy, including the Alpine regions — but this book deals only with the Lake District.

Comments by local people who met Wordsworth from time to time and who were later interviewed by Hardwicke Rawnsley indicate that he dressed modestly: 'whenever you met the poet he was sure to be quite plainly dressed. Sometimes in a round blue cloak; sometimes wearing a big wideawake, or a bit of an old boxer, but plainly dressed, almost poorly dressed at the best o' times.' Another witness comments on his having a cloak and umbrella on his frequent walks from Rydal to Ambleside. The same local sources claim that his walking preference was for roads, rough surfaced at the time. During one long walk from Yorkshire to the Lake District times and distances are quoted which indicate that he sustained a rate of slightly more than 6.5km (4 miles) per hour over a distance of several miles, a pace which many of us can only envy.

The itinerary of the tour with Coleridge provides abundant associations for the present purpose, but even more useful is the diary Wordsworth's sister Dorothy kept from 1800 to 1803. Dorothy was his closest companion throughout most of his life, an integral part of the Wordsworth household even after his marriage. It would be no exaggeration to say that she provided a large part of his inspiration and encouragement. Much has been made of the unusual closeness of this relationship, the diary entry for the day of William's wedding (with the later deletion of a passage concerning Dorothy wearing the wedding ring) often being cited as evidence. Unfortunately, the period from 23 December 1800 to 10 October 1801 is not covered; it is believed that a volume of the diary has been lost. Sadly, the diary faded away shortly after William's wedding, perhaps a victim of Dorothy's anguish at having to face a future in which she would have to share the love and attentions of her dear William.

Throughout his life Wordsworth produced an enormous quantity of poetry, including huge works such as *The Prelude* and shorter poems such as 'Michael', 'Daffodils' and the 'Duddon Sonnets', the shorter works often being more accessible to the non-specialist reader. Many of these outpourings contain geographical references which contribute to the associations used in selecting these walks.

In extolling Wordsworth as a poet it would be easy to overlook his one outstanding work of prose, his *Guide to the Lakes*, which first appeared in 1810 as an anonymous introduction to a volume of drawings by the Revd Joseph Wilkinson, a Norfolk clergyman. Wordsworth disliked the drawings and, ten years later, republished his text with some alterations. Further editions followed; today, the fifth edition, of 1835, with an introduction by Ernest de Selincourt, is regarded as the definitive version. This version includes chapters setting out the poet's forthright views on matters as diverse as building requirements, the layout of gardens and the danger to the Lake District that would result from the construction of the Kendal and Windermere railway. Indeed, after a short objective section, 'For the Tourist', the guide becomes a vehicle for Wordsworth's views on what is good and what is less good both for the district and also more widely. It is significant that it 'is intended as a Guide or Companion for the minds of Persons of taste, and feeling for the landscape'; the beauties of the Lake District would clearly, he thought, be wasted

Ann Tyson's Cottage, Hawkshead
PREVIOUS PAGES Lower Rydal Falls and the Viewing House

on the general public of the early nineteenth century. The guide was a great success, far outselling any of his poetry; according to de Selincourt it is 'a work instinct with the genius of a poet, who, though ready for the occasion to submit to the conditions of prose utterance,

is yet unable to abrogate his nature, but continually illuminates his subject with gleams of light that have a rarer source'.

Before the end of the nineteenth century he was already being described as 'the incomparable Wordsworth; the very personification of Lakeland; his memory is everywhere'.

Dove Cottage

In considering Wordsworth's present-day relevance, mention must be made of his incredible foresight. Although he would have been unlikely to have known the word 'conservationist', he was undoubtedly the first in a direct line which has since included John Ruskin, Canon Rawnsley, Beatrix Potter and countless others less well known. While his extreme views on such matters as railways and larches (which he violently disliked: in his *Guide to the Lakes* he waxes eloquent in analysing exactly what is wrong with planting them) now seem to be obsessive and almost comical, his ability to see beyond the immediate and to anticipate what might befall his beloved Lake District was truly prophetic.

In walking in his footsteps we should all be aware of the debt we owe this remarkable man: the conservation of the fragile landscape of the Lake District, discouraging inappropriate development, coupled with his understanding and enjoyment of the countryside, and the production for posterity of a large amount of outstanding poetry. And who knows, perhaps something of the spirit of Wordsworth, his incredible sensitivity to all things natural, will descend on at least some of us, heightening our understanding and consequent enjoyment of this marvellous countryside.

Dining room, Rydal Mount

1. GRASMERE VILLAGE

An entirely pleasant, gentle circular stroll which includes the centre of Grasmere village, Allan Bank and Butharlyp Howe. The only complication is that Easedale Beck is crossed on stepping stones, which is easy but possibly off-putting for some walkers. At least in summer, it is no hardship to paddle across. There are no stiles.

DISTANCE	5km (3 miles)
ASCENT	75m (246ft)
START/PARKING	Large lay-by on the east side of the A591, a short distance to the north of the roundabout, grid reference 342075. Alternatively, any of the pay-and-display car parks in Grasmere village.
REFRESHMENTS	Wide selection of inns and cafés in Grasmere village.
MAP	Ordnance Survey Explorer OL7, The English Lakes, south-eastern area, 1:25,000.

Stepping stones, Easedale Beck

THE WALK

Ⓢ Cross the A591 at the southern end of the lay-by to a little gate signposted 'public footpath Grasmere Village ½ mile via Millennium Bridge'. The excellent path has a stream on the left and fine views to Helm Crag on the right.

① At a signposted junction turn sharp right to cross the River Rothay on the Millennium Bridge, heading for 'Grasmere Village'. On the far side of the bridge turn left to head for 'Grasmere Church'.

② On reaching the village street, divert to the left, passing the Wordsworth Memorial Daffodil Garden and Sara Nelson's Gingerbread Shop. Turn left into the churchyard; the Wordsworth family graves are at the back, close to the river. Across the road from the church is the Old Rectory. Resuming the basic route, pass the Wordsworth Hotel and keep left to stay with the main street. Pass the Red Lion Hotel, and then go straight ahead along a cul-de-sac beside the Miller Howe Café. To the left is Silver Howe. Pass a 'National Trust, Allan Bank' sign. The private road rises steadily towards Allan Bank, a substantial house on high ground to the left.

③ At a fork 150m below the house keep right; there is a little 'path' sign with arrow. At a junction just before cottages keep right at the sign 'footpath to Goody Bridge'. Fifty metres beyond the cottages turn right, through a little gate, to take a path signposted to Goody Bridge. The narrow but clear path descends over grass. Ahead are Seat Sandal, and Fairfield and the mountains that form the famous horseshoe walk, separated by Grisedale Hause. Go through a kissing gate to reach the stepping stones across Easedale Beck. Cross by whatever means and ascend the far bank; pass a waymark on a post and go between the buildings of the former farm at Goody Bridge to join the Easedale Road.

④ Turn right, cross Goody Bridge, and then go through a little gate on the right to walk along a path beside the road. Rejoin the road through a little gate on the left. Turn right to follow the road for almost 100m. Turn left immediately after passing Silver Lea, through a signposted gate. Ascend gently through the Butharlyp Howe woodland, with the Easedale Beck and then the River Rothay below to the left.

⑤ Go through a gate to join the village street, turning left to cross the river. Turn right by Riversdale Guest House. There is a 'public footpath, Forest Side' sign on the wall. The path heads towards the Roman Catholic church on the far side of the A591. Join the A591, turning right.

⑥ After 60m leave the road, turning right through a gate to follow a signposted footpath towards Grasmere village. The track crosses meadows, with waymarked kissing gates, before rejoining the outward route close to the Millennium Bridge. Turn left to return to the car park.

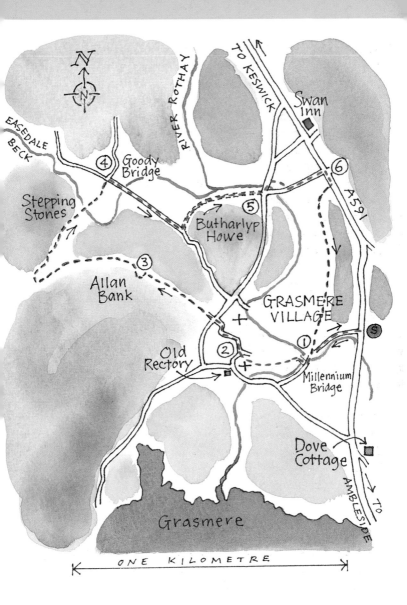

N

EASEDALE BECK

RIVER ROTHAY

TO KESWICK

Swan Inn

④ Goody Bridge

⑥

A591

Stepping Stones

⑤

Butharlyp Howe

③

Allan Bank

GRASMERE VILLAGE

S

①

② Old Rectory

Millennium Bridge

Dove Cottage

TO AMBLESIDE

Grasmere

ONE KILOMETRE

For many years Grasmere was central to the life of Wordsworth. Particularly during the years when he lived at Dove Cottage, he and his sister Dorothy, with or without other members of the family, often walked around Butharlyp Howe as a short stroll. Dorothy recorded these walks in her journal, with comments such as 'We walked on Butterlip How under the wind it rained all the while but we had a pleasant walk.'

After leaving Dove Cottage in 1808 Wordsworth and his expanding family moved to Allan Bank, a much bigger house prominently sited on a knoll above the village. In fact the site was so prominent that, a few years earlier, in 1805, when the house was constructed for a Liverpool merchant, Wordsworth had referred to it as a 'temple of abomination'. His need for larger accommodation obviously outweighed his aesthetic principles on this occasion and he planted trees to lessen the impact of the house when viewed from the village. The house was later occupied by Dr Thomas Arnold, headmaster of Rugby School, who became a friend of Wordsworth in his later years at Rydal.

Grasmere and Seat Sandal

In 1811 the Wordsworths moved again, this time to the Old Rectory in Grasmere, situated opposite the church. In 1813 they made a final move to Rydal Mount, approximately 3km (2 miles) away. The period at the Old Rectory was most unhappy: the house was dark and damp and two of the Wordsworth children, Catherine and Thomas, became seriously ill and died.

On his death, after thirty-seven years at Rydal, Wordsworth had a final Grasmere homecoming, being buried in the Grasmere churchyard, where he now lies, accompanied by several members of the family. He had previously planted eight yew trees here; one of them marks the graves of William and his wife, Mary.

From early days Wordsworth had made no secret of his love of the Grasmere area. As a schoolboy he had walked from Hawkshead to Grasmere, writing in *Home at Grasmere*:

> What happy fortune were it here to live!
> And if a thought of dying, if a thought
> Of mortal separation should come in
> With paradise before me, here to die.

In his view of the Grasmere Vale and its people he shared the view of Thomas Gray (of 'Elegy Written in a Country Churchyard' fame):

> Not a single red tile, no flaring gentleman's house,
>   or garden walls
> Break in upon the repose of this little unsuspected paradise:
> But all is peace, rusticity, and happy poverty, in its neatest,
> Most becoming attire.

2. GREENHEAD GILL AND ALCOCK TARN

This walk combines an exploration of the lower part of the Greenhead Gill valley near Grasmere with a circuit including Alcock Tarn. The tarn sits in a shallow depression at a height of 356m (1,170ft) on the flank of Heron Pike; from close to the tarn the views are splendidly wide-ranging. The ascent is quite steep but there are no difficulties. A stroll through Grasmere village with its many attractions, which are mentioned in walk 1, can be included as part of the return route.

Greenhead Gill

DISTANCE	5.5km (3½ miles)
ASCENT	330m (1,083ft)
START/PARKING	Roadside lay-by on the A591 a short distance to the north of the Swan Hotel (2-hour limit), grid reference 338085, or any Grasmere car park.
REFRESHMENTS	Wide choice in Grasmere.
MAP	Ordnance Survey Explorer OL7, The English Lakes, south-eastern area, 1:25,000.

THE WALK

S From the lay-by walk towards the Swan Hotel.

1 After approximately 100m turn left to follow a minor road. Pass the entrances to Michael's Nook and other properties. Turn left at a footpath signposted 'Greenhead Gill and Alcock Tarn', which soon rises steadily, with the rapid flow of Greenhead Gill on the right.

2 At a waymarked gate there are public footpaths to Stone Arthur (left) and to Alcock Tarn (right). Straight ahead, through the bracken, is a third path that keeps close to the side of the gill. To look for heaps of stones that are possibly the site of the sheepfold in Wordsworth's poem 'Michael', follow this path as far as the structure that carries the Manchester water conduit across the valley. This is a relatively short distance and there are certainly likely sites for the sheepfold evident.

3 Return to point 2 and commence the steady ascent towards Alcock Tarn, on a clear, well-used path. Pass below Butter Crag and a small pond/boggy area before going over a stile to reach the tarn. This is a fine picnic place.

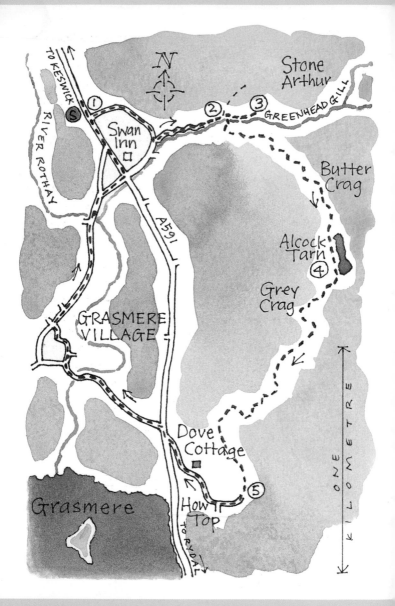

TO KESWICK

RIVER ROTHAY

N

Stone
Arthur

① ②

③ GREENHEAD GILL

Ⓢ

Swan
Inn

Butter
Crag

A591

Alcock
Tarn

④

Grey
Crag

GRASMERE
VILLAGE

Dove
Cottage

⑤

How
Top

TO RYDAL

Grasmere

ONE KILOMETRE

④ There are two routes down from the tarn. The first goes straight ahead to a stile and then continues downhill; it is steep and stony in places but always easy to follow. A more attractive route goes through a gap in the wall up to the right of the tarn, which is also the finest viewpoint: Windermere, Morecambe Bay, Coniston Old Man, Wetherlam, Crinkle Crags, Bowfell, the Langdale Pikes, Helm Crag and Steel Fell are all visible, with the Vale of Grasmere spread out below. From the gap a path loops round Grey Crag and crosses the Alcock Tarn outfall stream before passing through tree plantations in its steady descent. The two paths come together before reaching a surfaced road, with a well-sited seat above a small pond.

⑤ Turn right to descend to a minor road junction, keeping right, downhill, to pass Dove Cottage before reaching the main road. Cross over and follow Stock Lane to walk into Grasmere village. Go through the village, taking the exit road past the village hall towards the Swan Hotel. At the road junction turn left to return to the parking area. (A shorter return can be made by omitting the village and walking along the A591 roadside pavement/grass verge directly to the parking lay-by.)

Remains of an old sheepfold

The sad story of Michael seems to be embedded in local folklore. The elderly shepherd and his younger wife lived a frugal and hard-working life on their land above Grasmere. Quite late in life they had a son, Luke, an only child who grew up working on the land with his father. The intention was that he would succeed his father in due course; however, because of financial losses by a nephew, some of the land had to be sold and consequent financial difficulties made it highly desirable for the young man to go away to stay and work with another kinsman for a period in some unnamed city, to seek his fortune. The son's move went well at first, and he wrote encouraging letters to his parents, but later he 'gave himself to evil courses' and had to flee the country; the letters home ceased and the parents had no further word from him.

As a side occupation the shepherd had started to build a new sheepfold by the side of Greenhead Gill, initially with help from his son, laying a few stones at a time when pressures of other work permitted. After Luke's departure the old man continued to build the sheepfold, year after year, stone by stone, laying progressively fewer stones as time went on. Eventually he would go to the fold and lay not a single stone. The son never returned, the parents died, the land was sold out of the family and their cottage was demolished.

The story fascinated Wordsworth and became the subject of one of his most popular (and best?) poems. As early as October 1800, Dorothy records in her journal: 'We walked up Greenhead Gill in search of a sheepfold' and 'The sheepfold is falling away. It is built nearly in the form of a heart unequally divided.' One year later she writes: 'We went no further than Greenhead Gill to the sheepfold.' There are other entries which show that Wordsworth would often go alone from his home at Dove Cottage to the remains of the sheepfold, seeking inspiration and composing what later became 'Michael, a Pastoral Poem', which begins:

And to that hollow dell from time to time
Did he repair, to build the Fold of which
His flock had need 'tis not forgotten yet
The pity which was then in every heart
For the old Man — and 'tis believed by all
That many and many a day he thither went,
And never lifted up a single stone.

There, by the Sheepfold, sometimes was he seen
Sitting alone, or with his faithful Dog,
Then old, beside him, lying at his feet.
The length of full seven years, from time to time,
He at the building of this Sheepfold wrought,
And left the work unfinished when he died.
Three years, or little more, did Isabel
Survive her husband: at her death the estate
Was sold, and went into a stranger's hand.
The cottage which was named the EVENING STAR
Is gone — the ploughshare has been through the ground
On which it stood; great changes have been wrought
In all the neighbourhood: — yet the oak is left
That grew beside their door; and the remains
Of the unfinished Sheepfold may be seen
Beside the boisterous brook of Greenhead Ghyll.

The rocky outcrop above Greenhead Gill is Stone Arthur.
Very striking when seen from Grasmere, it is reached by a footpath
starting from the gate mentioned in the route to the sheepfold.
It is not really a peak in its own right, being merely an eminence
on the way to Great Dodd, one of the peaks of the group known
as the Fairfield horseshoe; nevertheless it was popular with the
Wordsworths; William and Dorothy loved the climb of what they
called 'William's Peak'.

3. EASEDALE TARN

A circular walk based on Grasmere, the outward route along the path that climbs up beside the Sourmilk Gill waterfalls to the beautifully situated Easedale Tarn. From the tarn a path across the upper part of Easedale connects with the Grasmere to Borrowdale track in Far Easedale for the return to Grasmere. Although the ascent is quite considerable, there are no really steep sections. A high proportion of the route is rough and stony underfoot.

DISTANCE	8km (5 miles)
ASCENT	240m (788ft)
START/PARKING	Choice in Grasmere village.
REFRESHMENTS	Inns and cafés in Grasmere. Teas at Lancrigg.
MAP	Ordnance Survey Explorer OL7, The English Lakes, south-eastern area, 1:25,000.

THE WALK

Ⓢ Leave Grasmere village along Easedale Road, opposite the bookshop. After approximately 300m look out for a little gate on the left, with a National Trust permissive path sign. Go through and follow the footpath behind the hedge until it rejoins the road just short of Goody Bridge. Cross the bridge and continue along the road.

① Just before the road peters out, turn left to cross the stream on a footbridge; there is a signpost to 'Easedale Tarn'. Pass a National Trust 'Easedale' sign, cross another bridge and follow a broad track heading into Easedale,

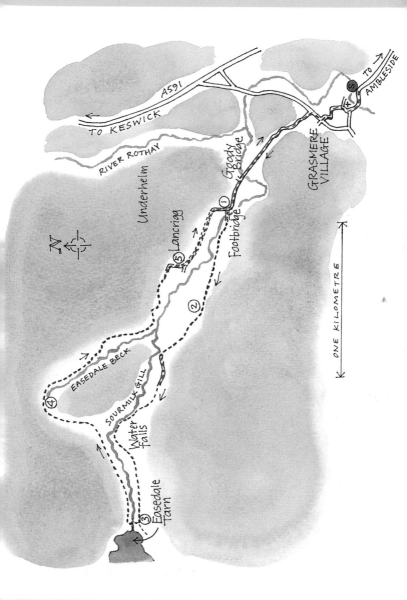

TO KESWICK

A591

RIVER ROTHAY

Underhelm

Lancrigg

Grasdale Bridge

Footbridge

GRASMERE VILLAGE

TO AMBLESIDE

S

N

EASEDALE BECK

SOURMILK GILL

Water Falls

Easedale Tarn

ONE KILOMETRE

① ② ③ ④ ⑤

EASEDALE TARN 27

Grasmere and Helm Crag

with the main waterfalls ahead and Helm Crag to the right. The track is rough and stony, improved in places, with the gill on the right.

② Cross a tributary stream on a concrete farm bridge, and then fork left at a 'public bridleway' sign; the path is now narrower, crossing a meadow before beginning to ascend beside the gill. Go through a kissing gate and continue along another improved section of path. The ascent is steady, the route never in doubt, passing beside an area of bog with cotton grass and an area obviously shaped by glacial action. There are lesser waterfalls in view below the outlet before you reach the tarn. Many years ago an entrepreneur provided a refreshment hut at this attractive but unlikely place; nowadays the excellent picnic spots have to suffice. Across the tarn is Greathead Crag; set back a little to its left is Tarn Crag; further to the left is Slapestone Edge. Far away, behind Helm Crag, Fairfield and the notch of Grisedale are prominent.

③ Opposite a large boulder turn right, along a little path heading for the foot of the tarn, which soon crosses Sourmilk Gill on easy stepping stones. Bear right to commence the descent, initially through bracken, parallel with the gill. The path continues to wind across the upper part of Easedale; it is always clear, improved in places and with stepping stones across several areas of boggy ground. Towards the far end there is a series of waymarks on posts and the path bears strongly to the left before joining the Far Easedale track.

④ Bear right to descend to a footbridge across Far Easedale Gill, and bear right again to follow this well-established track down the valley. Silver Howe can be seen to the right, ahead, and there is a particularly attractive section where the beck rushes along its rocky course. Pass outlying farm buildings and above a sizeable farm complex before entering woodland to reach a junction with the Helm Crag path. Go ahead at the 'Grasmere' signpost, and then through a gate.

⑤ Turn left at once, up a few steps and through a little gate to follow a woodland path towards Lancrigg, signposted 'Poet's Walk', with 'teas for walkers'. Pass two ponds and an information board before entering the Lancrigg gardens and passing below the front of the house. Go up a few steps to a parking area and continue along the Lancrigg access drive, crossing a track before leaving the Lancrigg grounds and rejoining the outward route by the end of the footbridge. Return to Grasmere village centre.

Readily accessed from Dove Cottage or either of Wordsworth's other two Grasmere homes, Easedale was prime country for shorter walks, mentioned several times in Dorothy's journal:

> They walked with us to see Churnmilk Force [Sour Milk Gill waterfall] and the Black Quarter. The Black Quarter looked marshy and the general prospect was cold, but the Force was very great.

> We set forward to walk into Easedale . . . we went up into Easedale and walked backwards and forwards in that flat field which makes the second circle of Easedale, with that beautiful rock in the field beside us and all the rocks and the woods and the mountains enclosing us round.

> We walked into Easedale — were turned back in the open field by the sight of a cow — every horned cow puts me in terror. We walked as far as we could, having crossed the footbridge, but it was dirty and we turned back.

The Wordsworth memorial drinking trough at Grasmere

Dove Cottage, Grasmere

To the Easedale Hills to hunt waterfalls. William and Mary left me sitting on a stone on the solitary mountains and went on to Easedale Tarn. I grew chilly and followed them. This approach to the tarn is very beautiful.

We walked into Easedale — sheltered in a cow-house — came home wet. The cuckow [sic] sang, and we watched the little birds as we sate [sic] at the door of the cow-house.

4. RYDAL AND GRASMERE

A delightful circular walk including both Rydal and Grasmere villages, using two of the most attractive footpaths in the Lake District: Loughrigg Terrace and the so-called 'Coffin Road'. Quite apart from the abundance of Wordsworth associations, this walk is well provided with interesting features. There are no severe ascents and no stiles, and the great majority of the route is excellent underfoot.

DISTANCE	9km (5½ miles)
ASCENT	150m (492ft)
START/PARKING	Roadside spaces along the cul-de-sac giving access to Rydal Church and Rydal Mount, grid reference 365062.
REFRESHMENTS	Café behind Rydal Hall; several inns and cafés in Grasmere.
MAP	Ordnance Survey Explorer OL7, The English Lakes, south-eastern area, 1:25,000.

THE WALK

S Start by walking up the road that passes Rydal Church, and then the entrance to Rydal Hall, before reaching the Rydal Mount car park. Continue to ascend past the car park to a junction with a 'public bridleway, Grasmere' sign. This is the start of the celebrated 'Coffin Road'.

Rydal Mount

① Turn left here, along a broad track that passes above Rydal Mount and its garden. Go through a waymarked gate, and then another gate, and continue along a delightful track across the hillside. Rydal Water comes into view; on the far side of the valley is the bulk of Loughrigg Fell; above, to the right, is the abrupt face of Nab Scar. There are more gates and a coffin resting stone before you reach a section that is rough underfoot; the track forks briefly here before widening and passing a house, Brockstone, on the right, and soon reaches tarmac. Pass a junction with a track to White Moss Common car park; then descend to a well-placed seat at a junction, with views over the Vale of Grasmere to Silver Howe.

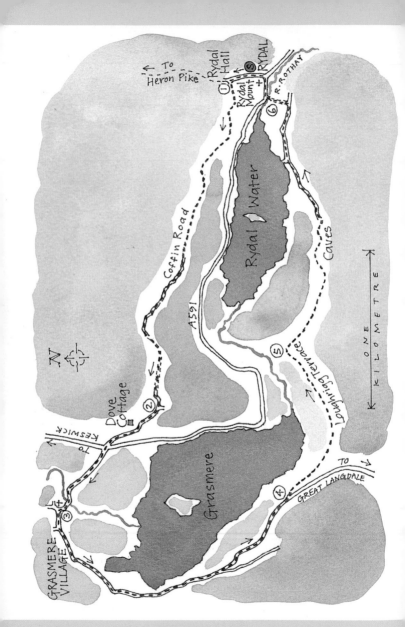

RYDAL

← To
Heron Pike

Rydal Hall

Rydal Mount

Rydal

R. ROTHAY

①

S

6

To KESWICK

Coffin Road

A591

Rydal Water

Caves

N

Dove Cottage

②

Loughrigg Terrace

⑤

Grasmere

④

TO GREAT LANGDALE

GRASMERE VILLAGE

③

ONE KILOMETRE

② Stay with the road, downhill; it soon joins another road, the former road between Grasmere and Rydal. Turn right to pass the old farm of How Top and continue downhill through the hamlet of Town End, to reach Dove Cottage, the museum and the Jerwood Centre. At the junction with the A591 main road, go across to walk along Stock Lane into Grasmere village. Cross the River Rothay and pass St Oswald's Church. The Wordsworth family graves are in the churchyard; the Old Rectory is opposite.

③ Turn left by the Grasmere Garden Centre (with spacious café) to follow Red Bank Road away from the village. Pass a junction and a car park, and then the Gold Rill Hotel. The lake comes into view by the Faeryland boating and refreshment centre. Stay with the road as it soon begins to rise steadily. At a fork keep left; there are fine views over the lake to Seat Sandal and the ridge leading to Fairfield. Pass Dale End Farm before reaching the start of the steepest section (25 per cent gradient).

④ As the road bears right, fork left, through a gate by a house. Unless you want to visit the shore of the lake, keep right, going slightly uphill, along the path signed 'public bridleway, Loughrigg Terrace and Rydal'. Enter Deerbolts Wood, following a fine wide track that rises through the woodland. At the top, go through a gate and turn left at a junction of tracks. Go through a kissing gate to reach the celebrated Loughrigg Terrace, a superb path across the flank of Loughrigg Fell. There are seats from which you can admire the lake, with a shingle beach, and an array of mountains. Blencathra can be seen through the gap of Dunmail Raise. At a fork, stay with the main path, which goes slightly downhill.

⑤ At a junction close to a wall bear right. At the next junction, in 20m, keep right again to follow a narrow path cutting across to join a more major path across the hillside after about 200m. Rydal Water is below as the track rises gently through bracken to a former (late nineteenth-century) slate quarrying area, with huge man-made caves. Continue downhill along the quarry access roadway. At the edge of woodland, by a gate, rake back sharp left for 50m; then turn sharp right at a seat to descend to the shore path of the lake. Bear right, through an old kissing gate, and take a clear track through the woodland. Leave the woodland at another old kissing gate before bearing left to cross the River Rothay on a footbridge. Go up to the A591 main road, opposite the Badger Bar.

⑥ Turn right for 150m and cross the road to return to the parking area.

The garden at Rydal Mount

This is truly William Wordsworth heartland. He lived at Dove Cottage from 1799 to 1808, at Allan Bank from 1808 to 1811 and at the Old Rectory from 1811 to 1813, all in Grasmere (the latter two homes are included in walk 1.) He worshipped at St Oswald's Church and is buried in the adjacent graveyard.

The period at Dove Cottage is of paramount importance in any appreciation of Wordsworth's life and work. After years of living in London, the West Country and Germany and wandering extensively in France, Switzerland and Italy, the vigorous and radical young poet had come home to his beloved Lake District, to set up house with his devoted sister Dorothy. The initial domestic discomforts he mentioned in a letter to Coleridge (it was a cold and wet December, the house was not in good repair and at least one of the fireplaces smoked badly; not surprisingly, both William and Dorothy caught 'troublesome colds') paled into insignificance beside the joy of homecoming. Nature's beauties were all around; there was a garden with orchard to tend; there were agreeable neighbours; there were roads and paths to walk; and poetry flowed from William unfettered.

After William's marriage to Mary Hutchinson in 1802, she and her sister joined the happy household, which was enriched by visits from Wordsworth's brother John and friends such as Coleridge and the novelist Walter Scott. The road from Grasmere to Rydal passed in front of the cottage before rising past How Top. Walking over to Rydal was almost an everyday occurrence for one or more of the household, often for the purpose of taking or collecting post. Walks across to Loughrigg were also frequent.

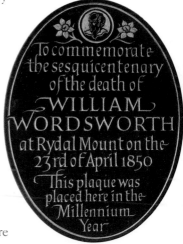

To commemorate the sesquicentenary of the death of WILLIAM WORDSWORTH at Rydal Mount on the 23rd of April 1850 This plaque was placed here in the Millennium Year

The lengthy residence at Rydal Mount, 1813 to 1850, was quite different. The former radical poet, perhaps saddened by the deaths of two of his children, had become altogether less ardent and his poetry arguably more laboured. He gradually became regarded as an establishment figure; he accepted a government post as Collector of Stamps for the area (a form of taxation) and, eventually, became Poet Laureate. Well before the end of his life in 1850, Dorothy suffered severe mental and physical decline while they were at Rydal.

Dove Cottage, together with an adjacent museum, is open to the public as a visitor attraction, and is an essential visit for anyone with an interest in Wordsworth and/or early nineteenth-century Lakeland. Close by is the Jerwood Centre, a fine modern research building with an immense collection of Wordsworth material.

Likewise, the altogether grander house at Rydal Mount, with its attractive and spacious gardens, is open to the public. By the side of the Rydal Mount access road, Rydal Church, built by Lady le Fleming of Rydal Hall in 1823/4, has a Wordsworth family pew. Behind the church is Dora's Field, which Wordsworth purchased when his landlady, Lady le Fleming, threatened him with eviction in 1826. In the event, he stayed at Rydal Mount, giving the field (see pages 44–5) to his daughter Dora, who died prematurely in 1847. William and Mary planted the field with daffodils.

5. AMBLESIDE, RYDAL AND UNDER LOUGHRIGG

An easy circuit linking Ambleside and Rydal, passing through the parkland of Rydal Hall, with a return along the minor road at the foot of Loughrigg. There are good mountain views. There are no stiles and all tracks are first rate. The walk includes a comparatively short section of the main road from Ambleside, with roadside footpath.

Rydal Hall, former home of the le Fleming family, has been used as a retreat centre by the Diocese of Carlisle for many years. Although there is only one right of way through the complex, the resident community are very visitor friendly and there are helpful information boards. The gardens, designed by Thomas Mawson, have been extensively refurbished in recent years. The Lower Rydal Falls, with their historic 'viewing house' of 1669, were admired by Constable and Turner and painted by Joseph Wright of Derby. Also in the grounds of the hall are two great blocks of stone sculpted by the late Josefina de Vasconcellos.

DISTANCE	5.5km (3½ miles)
ASCENT	Negligible
START/PARKING	Main pay-and-display car park in Rydal Road, at the north end of Ambleside, grid reference 376047.
REFRESHMENTS	Tea shop behind Rydal Hall.
MAP	Ordnance Survey Explorer OL7, The English Lakes, south-eastern area, 1:25,000.

Lower Rydal Falls

THE WALK

S Starting from the car park turn left along the road towards Grasmere. Opposite the car park is the attractive Ambleside campus of the University of Cumbria, still known locally as Charlotte Mason College.

① After less than 0.75km (½ mile), just after crossing Scandale Beck, cross the road to an obvious lodge, with iron gates and a footpath signposted to 'Rydal Hall'. (There is a bus stop close to this point that could be used – 555 and 599 services – to avoid walking along the roadside.) Follow the broad track rising very gently through the parkland to the hall. Ahead is the Nab at the end of the ridge that leads to Fairfield and the famous horseshoe walk. Across the valley is the bulk of Loughrigg, with Crinkle Crags and Bowfell peeping through the gap above Red Bank. As it approaches the hall the track passes through light and well-varied woodland, with some good specimen trees.

② At a junction close to the hall, the well-signposted path turns right, uphill. A short left diversion at this point gives a view of the Lower Rydal Falls. The signposted path passes between outbuildings of the hall and over the Rydal Beck; there is a turbine to the right of the beck which supplies electricity to the complex. To the right is the Old Schoolroom Tea Shop. The gardens, in front of the hall, may be accessed either before or after passing behind the building.

③ Join the road just below Rydal Mount (a cul-de-sac) and turn left to descend past the church to the main road. Turn left along the roadside pavement for a short distance.

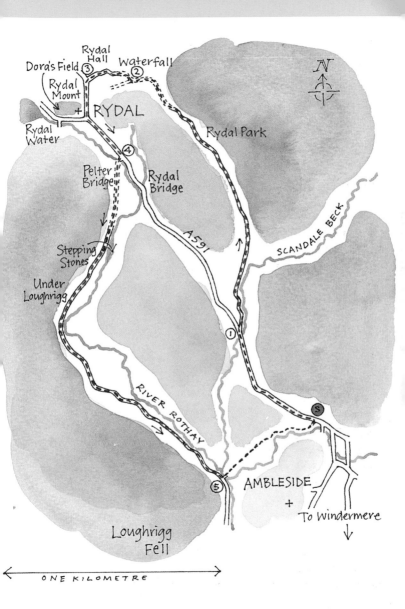

Rydal Hall

Dora's Field

Waterfall ②

③

Rydal Mount

✝ RYDAL

Rydal Water

④

Rydal Park

N

Pelter Bridge

Rydal Bridge

A591

Stepping Stones

Under Loughrigg

SCANDALE BECK

①

RIVER ROTHAY

Ⓢ

⑤

AMBLESIDE

✝

To Windermere

Loughrigg Fell

← ONE KILOMETRE →

④ Turn right to cross the River Rothay over Pelter Bridge and follow the Under Loughrigg road, initially across the water meadows, for about 2km (1¼ miles). This quiet road provides a pleasant walking route, with views of the river, Wansfell Pike, Snarker Pike and Red Screes. Part way along are stepping stones across the river. The path also passes Fox How, built by Dr Arnold, the headmaster of Rugby School, below the road to the left.

Dora's Field, Rydal

⑤ Turn left to leave the road over a shapely (packhorse?) bridge across the river. Either go straight ahead to return directly to Rydal Road and the car park or fork right to cross Stockghyll Beck and Rothay Park, passing the church on the way into Ambleside.

Loughrigg Fell and its surrounding area were well known to the Wordsworths, within very easy reach of their later home at Rydal. The Wordsworth assocations with Rydal, Rydal Mount and Rydal Church are described in walk 4. Loughrigg is at no great distance from Dove Cottage and the Wordsworths' other Grasmere houses. In her journal Dorothy mentions ascending to the summit of the fell, and compares the relative beauty of Rydal Water and Grasmere.

In his *Guide to the Lakes* William recommends, from Ambleside, 'the ride, or walk by Rothay Bridge, and up the stream under Loughrigg Fell'. In May 1800, Dorothy twice mentions coming home from Ambleside by Clappersgate, obviously along the Under Loughrigg road. From Grasmere to Ambleside and back was a frequent evening excursion. On 2 June 1800 she writes: 'I went to Ambleside after tea, crossed the stepping stones at the foot of Grasmere, and pursued my way on the other side of Ryedale and by Clappersgate'; and not surprisingly, 'It was near 11 when

Wordsworth-style chimneys

Rydal Church

I reached home.' On 15 October 1801, William and Dorothy 'walked up Loughrigg Fell then by the waterside'. Several references to stepping stones appear to refer to a set close to Grasmere; those passed on this walk give an idea of the kind of river crossing available to the Wordsworths.

In his *Guide to the Lakes*, Wordsworth describes in great detail what features he thought should be incorporated in house design in the district. 'Nor will the singular beauty of the chimneys escape the eye of the attentive traveller . . . Others are of a quadrangular shape, rising one or two feet above the roof; which low square is often surmounted by a tall cylinder, giving to the cottage chimney the most beautiful shape in which it is ever seen.' Dr Arnold built Fox How with advice from his friend and neighbour William Wordsworth. As would be expected, the chimneys have the recommended combination of square bases and cylindrical upper portions.

6. LOUGHRIGG TARN

A pleasant, undemanding, short stroll, suitable for all
categories of walker, around a lovely little tarn situated
beneath the steep slopes of Loughrigg Fell. There is
no significant ascent and no difficulty underfoot.

DISTANCE	3km (1¾ miles)
ASCENT	15m (49ft)
START/PARKING	Two small roadside parking areas close to the junction of minor roads to the south of the tarn, grid reference 346040. To reach the parking area from the Ambleside to Coniston and Great Langdale road, turn right towards Grasmere at Ellers Brow, just over 1.5km (1 mile) beyond Clappersgate.
REFRESHMENTS	None en route. Skelwith Bridge Hotel and the café at the slate works showrooms are close by.
MAP	Ordnance Survey Explorer OL7, The English Lakes, south-eastern area, 1:25,000.

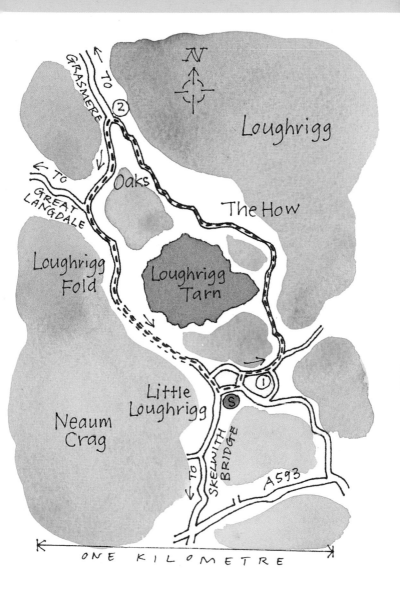

THE WALK

(S) Starting from either parking place walk back along the access road, downhill, crossing a small stream on a road bridge.

(1) After 40m turn left along a track heading for cottages and towards the peak of Loughrigg. After 50m fork right at a waymarked junction, to pass in front of the cottages. At the next junction go left, through a gate beside Tarn Foot Lodge. Take the broad, easy, level track that meanders along the base of Loughrigg, passing a camping site on the left, with the tarn soon in sight. The views across to Wetherlam, Bowfell and the Langdale Pikes are superb. Pass The How, an old farmstead with attractive buildings and garden.

The How, Loughrigg

The Oaks, Loughrigg

② Join a minor road, turning sharp left to walk past another old farmstead, The Oaks, with lovely bank barns by the side of the road. Keep left at a road junction, signposted to 'Ambleside and Coniston'; continue along the roadside, with Loughrigg as the dominant view and little Neaum Crag up to the right, to complete the circuit and return to the parking place.

Reviewing tarns in his *Guide to the Lakes*, Wordsworth writes:

A Tarn in a Vale implies, for the most part, that the bed of the vale is not happily formed; that the water of the brooks can neither wholly escape, nor diffuse itself over a large area. Accordingly, in such situations, Tarns are often surrounded by an unsightly tract of boggy ground; but this is not always the case, and in the cultivated parts of the country, when the shores of the Tarn are determined, it differs only from the Lake in being smaller, and in belonging mostly to a smaller valley, or circular recess. Of this class of miniature lakes,

Loughrigg Tarn, near Grasmere, is the most beautiful example. It has a margin of green firm meadows, of rocks, and rocky woods, a few reeds here, a little company of water lilies there, with beds of gravel or stone beyond; a tiny stream issuing neither briskly nor sluggishly out of it; but its feeding rills, from the shortness of their course, so small as to be scarcely visible. Five or six cottages are reflected in its peaceful bosom; rocky and barren steeps rise up above the hanging enclosures; and the solemn pikes of Langdale overlook, from a distance, the low cultivated ridge of land that forms the northern boundary of this small, quiet, and fertile domain.

Boat on Loweswater

7. BLEA TARN

The minor road connecting the Great and Little
Langdale valleys climbs steeply to a pass at the foot of
Side Pike. Before the start of the descent into Little
Langdale is a generally flat area, with the lovely little
Blea Tarn at the foot of the steep slopes of Blake Rigg,
rising to Pike O'Blisco behind.

This circuit of the tarn makes a very easy and
attractive ramble, outwards on a wide track, with the
return along the minor road.

DISTANCE	2.5km (1½ miles)
ASCENT	30m (98ft)
START/PARKING	Small National Trust car park by the roadside, opposite Blea Tarn, grid reference 296043.
REFRESHMENTS	None en route. Inns in both the Langdale valleys.
MAP	Ordnance Survey Explorer OL6, The English Lakes, south-western area, 1:25,000.

THE WALK

🅢 Starting from the car park cross the road to a gate.
Go through and follow the broad track towards the
near end of the tarn. To the right the Langdale Pikes
are beautifully framed between the shoulders of Kettle
Crag and Side Pike. Pike O'Stickle, Gimmer Crag, Loft
Crag, Thorn Crag and Harrison Stickle are all in view.

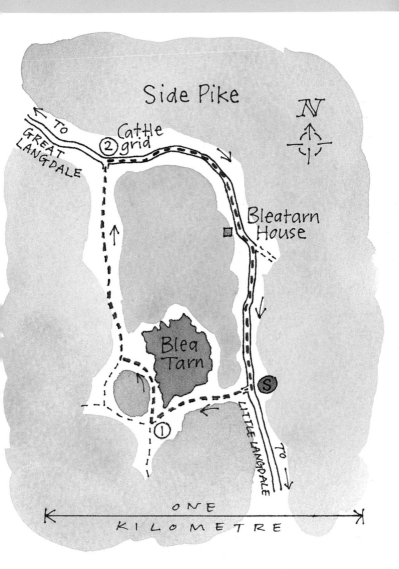

Side Pike

N

To GREAT LANGDALE

Cattle grid ②

Bleatarn House

Blea Tarn

S

①

To LITTLE LANGDALE

ONE KILOMETRE

① Cross the outfall stream by the footbridge and turn right at once to continue through the predominantly coniferous woodland, quite close to the shore of the tarn. The path emerges from the woodland on the open fell side, with a superb view now ahead, heading

Blea Tarn and the Langdale Pikes

unmistakably towards the highest point of the road, with a cattle grid, reached through a gate.

② Turn right to return along the road to the car park (or retrace by the same route if the road is busy).

As he described in *The Excursion*, William and his brother John climbed in the mountains above Langdale and circled Blea Tarn:

We scaled without a track to ease our steps,
A steep ascent; and reached a dreary plain,
With a tumultuous waste of huge hill tops
Before us, savage region! which I paced
Dispirited: when, all at once, behold!
Beneath our feet, a little lowly vale,
A lowly vale, and yet uplifted high
Among the mountains; even as if the spot
Had been taken from eldest time by wish of theirs
So placed, to be shut out from all the world!
Urn like it was in shape, deep as an urn;
With rocks encompassed, save that to the south
Was one small opening, where a heath clad ridge
Supplied a boundary less abrupt and close;
A quiet treeless nook, with two green fields,
A liquid pool that glittered in the sun,
And one bare dwelling; one abode, no more!
It seemed the home of poverty and toil,
Though not of want: the little fields, made green
By husbandry of many thrifty years,
Paid cheerful tribute to the moorland house.
— There crows the cock, single in his domain:
The small birds find in spring no thicket there
To shade them; only from the neighbouring vales
The cuckoo, straggling up to the hill tops,
Shouteth faint tidings of some gladder place.

. . . full many a spot
Of hidden beauty have I chanced to espy
Among the mountains; never one like this
So lonesome, and so perfectly secure.

William Wordsworth as a young man

8. HAWKSHEAD

A circuit that starts and finishes at Hawkshead Moor, part of the huge Grizedale Forest. At roughly the mid-point of the route is Hawkshead village, a compact old settlement of charming little squares and alleyways and a very popular centre for visitors, best visited on foot. Of particular interest are the church, the ancient former grammar school, the Beatrix Potter Gallery and Ann Tyson's Cottage.

Grizedale Forest is a large area of commercial woodland, owned and managed by Forest Enterprises. For many years it has been walker (and cyclist) friendly. There is a comprehensive visitor centre about 1.5km (1 mile) further along the minor road from the recommended car park. The place names Roger Ground and Walker Ground date from the time of the dissolution of the monasteries by Henry VIII in 1539/40. Parcels of the land then owned by the great Furness Abbey were sold off to individuals, whose names have endured over the subsequent centuries.

Generally good tracks and footpaths throughout; one short length of public road.

DISTANCE	6.5km (4 miles)
ASCENT	165m (443ft)
START/PARKING	Moor Top Forest Enterprises car park (free) with picnic tables, well signposted from the minor road connecting Hawkshead and Grizedale, via Roger Ground, grid reference 344965.
REFRESHMENTS	Choice of inns and cafés in Hawkshead.
MAP	Ordnance Survey Explorer OL7, The English Lakes, south-eastern area, 1:25,000.

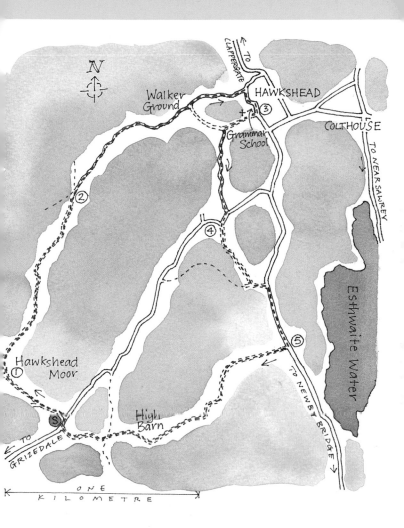

N

Walker Ground

HAWKSHEAD

③

TO CLAPPERGATE

TO

COLTHOUSE

+ Grammar School

TO NEAR SAWREY

②

④

⑤

Esthwaite Water

Hawkshead Moor

①

Ⓢ

TO GRIZEDALE

High Barn

TO NEWBY BRIDGE

ONE KILOMETRE

THE WALK

(S) Walk past the vehicular barrier at the back of the car park. At a multi-waymarked and signposted junction after 25m – 'public bridleway, Hawkshead, 1¾ miles' – go straight ahead, passing through attractively mixed woodland.

(1) At a three-way junction after approximately 200m turn right to follow a broad forest road, more or less level for almost 1.25km (¾ mile).

(2) Turn right to leave the forest road at the 'public bridleway, Hawkshead ¾ mile' signpost. Follow the good track that descends steadily towards the village, with a wall, and then a stream, on the right. There are excellent mountain views. You soon reach the buildings of Walker Ground, with a 'Hawkshead' signpost and tarmac underfoot. Continue along Vicarage Lane, passing Ann Tyson's Cottage, to reach the village centre. Turn right to follow the main street as far as a little green, by the information centre and public conveniences. The various Hawkshead attractions are closely grouped.

The Old Grammar School, Hawkshead

③ Turn right to pass the front of the former grammar school and rise steeply through the churchyard, bearing left to a gate at the far boundary. Note the particularly good example of the local traditional slate-on-edge walling. At the next gate, in 70m, turn left at a 'Roger Ground' signpost. Follow the narrow but clear path, through more gates, to reach the hamlet of Roger Ground. Turn right and walk along the steeply rising minor road for 100m.

④ Turn left at a signposted road junction to take the 'footpath Howe Farm', which goes initially downhill on tarmac. Pass Springfield, cross a little footbridge and follow a narrow but clear grass path direct to Howe Farm, with Esthwaite Water in view. Pass the farm to the left, through two gates, to join the farm access road. Turn left to walk to the public road in 50m. Turn right and walk by the roadside for almost 400m.

⑤ Turn right at the second of two adjacent access drives, with a 'public footpath' sign. Pass through a small hamlet with old buildings and through the grounds of the last house, Elder Ghyll, to a waymarked gate to the left of the house. Go through the gate to commence the long ascent back to Moor Top, crossing a lively stream on a footbridge and ascending along the side of an attractive wooded valley. Leave the woodland at a gate, cross a stream on a tiny footbridge and continue the ascent across open countryside, bearing left and following occasional waymarks on posts. There is some wet ground and several gates before the path reaches the isolated dwelling High Barn. Pass between the house and its outbuilding to continue along the access drive, which ascends steadily to join the Hawkshead to Grizedale road, passing a 'Moor Top' signpost en route. At the road turn right to return to the car park in a few metres.

For eight years Wordsworth attended Hawkshead Grammar School, founded in 1585 by Edwin Sandys, Archbishop of York. He joined the school in May 1779 with his eleven-year-old brother Richard. They were later joined by his other two brothers, John and Christopher. During his time at the school he lodged with Ann and Hugh Tyson, until 1783 at the well-known cottage in Hawkshead, and then at nearby Colthouse. Ann was widowed in 1784.

Wordsworth's mother had died before he came to Hawkshead and his father died fairly suddenly in 1783. Undoubtedly, Ann Tyson's motherly care helped the young boy to cope with being an orphan. Throughout his life he remembered her with great affection, writing:

> The thoughts of gratitude shall fall like dew
> Upon thy grave, good creature! While my heart
> Can beat I never will forget thy name.

By all accounts the quality of the teaching at the school provided a good foundation for his achievements in later life; perhaps most importantly he was encouraged to write. One of the prime exhibits at the school is a desk with his initials carved into the wood.

While during his leisure time he sometimes joined his fellow pupils in organized games, boating on Windermere and skating on Esthwaite Water, he also found time to be alone, 'wandering half the night among the cliffs' or rising early in the morning to climb the local hillsides.

He left Hawkshead to go to Cambridge University in 1787 but returned to stay with Ann Tyson in 1788 and 1789 for his first two summer vacations, still regarding the village as his home. During his 1799 walking tour with Coleridge, he again returned to Hawkshead, three years after Ann Tyson's death, once more expressing his gratitude to the simple old woman whom he and his brothers honoured 'with little less than filial love'.

PREVIOUS PAGES Hawkshead village

The gentle Esthwaite Water was always a favourite with Wordsworth. Apart from enjoying it for the ice skating, in 'An Evening Walk' he included it among the 'fair scenes' he remembers of his youth in the Lake District:

> Where twilight glens endear my Esthwaite's shore,
> And memory of departed pleasures, more.

For closer acquaintance with Esthwaite's shore, there is a footpath that leaves the road to the south of Hawkshead, opposite the junction with the road to Grizedale.

Wordsworth Street, Hawkshead

9. CLAIFE HEIGHTS AND THE WINDERMERE SHORE

This circular walk visits the ruins of Thomas West's 'viewing station', erected in the 1790s, and then climbs to the top of Claife Heights before descending gently to the lake shore and returning along the little road by the side of the lake.

Author of the best-known early guide to the Lake District (1778), Thomas West selected viewpoints or 'stations' from which visitors could enjoy scenic views. The Claife 'station' provided pleasure rooms which remained fashionable for parties and dances well into the nineteenth century. The drawing room had three windows of different-coloured glass, each giving the impression of seeing the lake and its surroundings in a different season.

The initial ascent is quite demanding; sections of the path are rough underfoot. There are no stiles.

DISTANCE	4km (2½ miles)
ASCENT	160m (525ft)
START/PARKING	National Trust pay-and-display car park on the right of the road leading from the ferry to Hawkshead, grid reference 388955.
REFRESHMENTS	Picnics only.
MAP	Ordnance Survey Explorer OL7, The English Lakes, south-eastern area, 1:25,000.

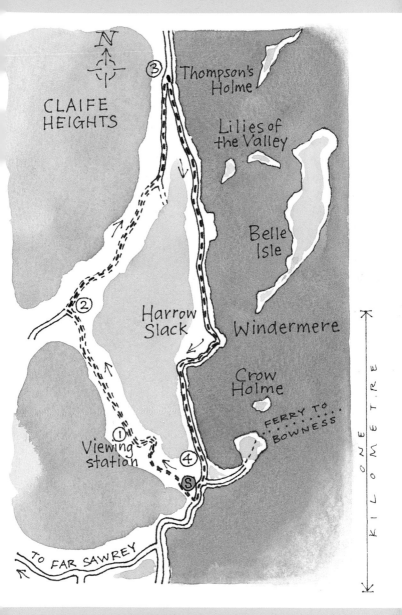

N

CLAIFE HEIGHTS

③ Thompson's Holme

Lilies of the Valley

Belle Isle

② Harrow Slack

Windermere

Crow Holme

FERRY TO BOWNESS

① Viewing station

④ ⑤

TO FAR SAWREY

KILOMETRE

THE WALK

S Start at the rear of the car park. Follow the 'public footpath ferry and Latterbarrow via Claife Station' signpost. At a junction after 100m there is another signpost; turn left here up a flight of stone steps. At the next signpost head for 'Claife, white post route', which within a short distance ascends to the ruins of the building at the viewing station.

① The path continues to rise – some sections of it rough underfoot – diagonally up the well-wooded hillside. Near the top is a signpost; keep right for 'Hawkshead'. There are glimpses of the lake through the trees as the path follows the top of Claife Heights. Cross a tiny stream and continue along the side of an old stone wall to reach a gate and a junction.

② Turn right to head for 'Lake Shore' along a broad, easy bridleway. Go through another gate to begin the long steady descent through varied woodland.

③ Join the lakeside roadway just north of the gate that marks the limit of public vehicular access. Turn sharp right to go through the gate and follow the

Windermere

cul-de-sac along the lake shore with fine views of islands – Thompson's Holme and the Lilies of the Valley, with Belle Isle behind – and of the Bowness area on the far shore. There are many excellent picnic spots along the shore. Pass the entrance to Harrow Slack and then the Harrow Slack car park.

④ Join the road that leads from the ferry to Hawkshead, the B5285. Turn right; after 10m there is a signposted footpath on the right which leads, with some ascent, to the top of the flight of steps used at the start of the walk. A left turn here leads directly back to the car park. Alternatively, walk a little further along the road before turning right; another little path leads directly into the car park, without the ascent.

Wordsworth was undoubtedly fond of Windermere, which in his day was free of the pressures of heavy use and mass tourism of more recent years that have resulted from its easy accessibility. In his *Guide to the Lakes* he writes:

> The Troutbeck Mountains about sunset make a splendid landscape. The view from the Pleasure-house of the Station near the Ferry has suffered much from Larch plantations; this mischief, however, is gradually disappearing, and the Larches, under the management of the proprietor, Mr. Curwen, are giving way to the native wood. Windermere ought to be seen both from its shores and from its surface. None of the other lakes unfold so many fresh beauties to him who sails upon them. This is owing to its greater size, to the islands, and to its having two vales at the head.

His poem 'There Was a Boy' sums up his boyhood feelings on evening visits to the lake:

Windermere and the Langdale Pikes

There was a boy, ye knew him well, ye cliffs
And islands of Winander! Many a time,
At evening, when the stars had just begun
To move along the edges of the hills,
Rising or setting, would he stand alone,
Beneath the trees, or by the shimmering lake;
And there, with fingers interwoven, both hands
Pressed closely palm to palm and to his mouth
Uplifted, he, as though an instrument,
Blew mimic hootings to the silent owls
That they might answer him. And they would shout
Across the watery vale, and shout again
Responsive to his call, with quivering peals,
And long halloos, and screams, and echoes loud.

Dorothy, too, appreciated it. On 8 June 1802, she rode to
Windermere and wrote:

I was enchanted with some of the views. From the High
Ray [Wray] the view is very delightful, rich, and festive,
water and wood, houses, groves, hedgerows, green fields, and
mountains, white houses, large and small . . . We put up our
horses, ate our dinner by the water-side and walked up to the
Station. Then we went to the Island, walked round it, and
crossed the lake with our horse in the ferry.

From the passage that follows it is clear, though, that she much
disliked the house that had fairly recently been built on Belle Isle:
'And that great house! Mercy upon us! If it could be concealed it
would be well for all who are not pained to see the pleasantest of
earthly spots deformed by man. But it cannot be covered. Even the
tallest of our old oak trees would not reach to the top of it.'

10. THIRLMERE

A short, simple walk by the shore of the south end of Thirlmere, with excellent waterside picnic spots. Beneath the lake is the site of the tiny hamlet of Wythburn, including two inns, which was destroyed and submerged when Manchester Corporation dammed the north end of the lake in the early 1890s, raising the water level by about 50 feet and constructing a pipeline to supply water to the city. Recent felling of some of the thousands of dull conifers planted by the Corporation has improved the appearance of Thirlmere and its environment, particularly as seen from the A591 main road. Trim little seventeenth-century Wythburn Church, higher up the hillside than its hamlet, has survived.

DISTANCE	3.25km (2 miles)
ASCENT	40m (130ft)
START/PARKING	Small pay-and-display car park at Steel End, less than 0.75km (½ mile) along the minor road from its junction with the A591 at the south end of Thirlmere, grid reference 321130.
REFRESHMENTS	Picnic only.
MAP	Ordnance Survey Explorer OL5, The English Lakes, north-eastern area, 1:25,000.

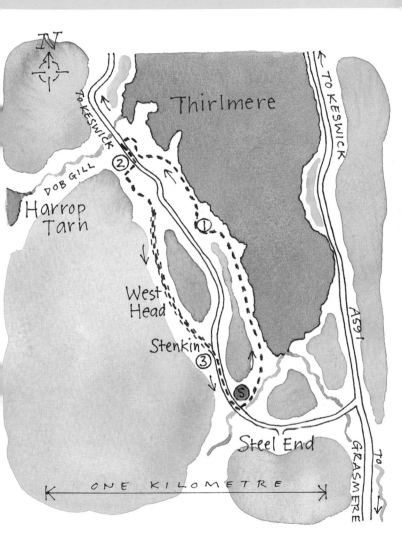

N

Thirlmere

TO KESWICK

TO KESWICK

DOB GILL

Harrop
Tarn

②

①

West
Head

Stenkin

③

Ⓢ

Steel End

A591

GRASMERE

TO

K —— ONE KILOMETRE —— >

THE WALK

(S) Start at the entrance to Steel End car park. A fingerpost points the way to Dob Gill, by a permissive path. Leaving the car park at the far end, go through a small gate and head for the lake shore. The path is not heavily used, but it is always clear as it winds its way through an area of generally wild vegetation. Helvellyn dominates the view in front as you approach the lake shore, with the rapids of Whelpside Gill showing up well in wet weather. There are many boardwalks as the path twists and turns through boggy ground.

(1) At a T-junction turn right. The path goes slightly downhill, soon reaching the ruins of a long-demolished building. By the ruins there is a waymark on a post. Pass between walls before ascending to join the road at a kissing gate. (Dob Gill car park, with public conveniences, is a short distance to the right.)

(2) Turn left, along the roadside, for about 300m. Turn right at a gate signposted 'Bridleway to Watendlath' along a grass track rising to a waymarked gate. The track is not well worn but it is easy to follow. Bear left after the gate; the path still ascends gently, with a wall close on the left. Steel Fell is dominant in the view ahead. The overview of the land between road and reservoir gives hints of how the valley would have looked, with comparatively good farming land, before the changes of the 1890s. Pass the ruins of a farm (West Head). Pass a signpost and continue on, now gently downhill, with a wall close on the left. Go through a gate, pass to the left of more farm buildings (Stenkin) and rejoin the road.

(3) Turn right to return along the roadside to the car park.

Wythburn Church and mountains

The Wordsworths often visited the Wythburn area, either en route to Keswick to visit the Coleridge family or using it as a place to meet Coleridge, approximately halfway between their respective homes. Before the dam was constructed there were two, much smaller, lakes, Wythburn Water and Leathes Water, with a connecting waterway crossed by a series of bridges. On 4 May 1802 Dorothy records: 'It was very hot . . . we were almost melted before we were at the top of the hill [Dunmail Raise]. We saw Coleridge on the Wythburn side of the water; he crossed the beck to us.'

Of particular significance to them was 'Sara's Crag' or 'Sara's Rock', later known as the Rock of Names, which they used as a rendezvous. Dorothy mentions it on several occasions, writing for instance on 4 May 1803: 'We parted from Coleridge at Sara's Crag, after having looked at the letters which Coleridge carved in the morning. I kissed them all. William deepened the T. with C's pen knife.' The letters that Coleridge carved were the initials of William Wordsworth, Dorothy Wordsworth, Mary Hutchinson (later William's wife), Sara Hutchinson (her sister), John Wordsworth

and Samuel Coleridge. Unfortunately the Rock of Names was destroyed during the construction of the reservoir in the early 1890s.

In his *Guide to the Lakes* Wordsworth advised travellers from Grasmere to Keswick to take a deviation from the main road in order to see to advantage Thirlmere, or Wythburn Lake, with its surrounding mountains. 'Having previously enquired at the Inn near Wythburn Chapel, the best way from this milestone to the bridge that divides the Lake, he must cross it, and proceed with the Lake on the right.'

Thirlmere in winter

11. WYTHBURN TO KESWICK

A linear route from Wythburn Church to the centre of
Keswick, quite long but with no serious ascent, generally
good tracks and footpaths, and a little roadside walking.
It is excellent scenically, with the views of and around
Thirlmere improved by tree felling; along the Naddle
valley Skiddaw and Blencathra may both be seen to
advantage. The excellent bus service from Keswick to
Lancaster (555) provides the return to Wythburn and is
also useful if only part of this route is undertaken.

Wordsworth purists can include more of his walk from
Grasmere by starting the walk along a footpath on the
right at the top of Dunmail Raise, crossing a footbridge
and joining the forest road to reach the starting point of
this walk, adding 2km (1 ¼ miles) to the overall distance.

DISTANCE	18.5km (11½ miles)
ASCENT	200m (656ft)
START/PARKING	Small car park at Wythburn Church, to the east of the A591 on the Thirlmere side of Dunmail Raise, grid reference 324136.
REFRESHMENTS	Good choice in Keswick.
MAPS	Ordnance Survey Explorer OL4 and OL5, The English Lakes, north-eastern and north-western areas, 1:25,000.

The dam at Thirlmere

THE WALK

Ⓢ At an opening in the wall at the far end of the car park go through a kissing gate to join a path, turning right to commence the ascent, with a stream on the left. There are views along Thirlmere as the stony track ascends steadily to join a forest roadway at a signpost.

① Turn left to head for 'Swirls'. Continue along the roadway, by permission of United Utilities, who have provided waymarks. (For many years Manchester Corporation, who planted this hillside with thousands of dull conifers, completely excluded the public on the grounds of protecting the purity of the water in their reservoir, Thirlmere.) The peak of Skiddaw comes into view ahead before the road ends; behind are Steel Fell

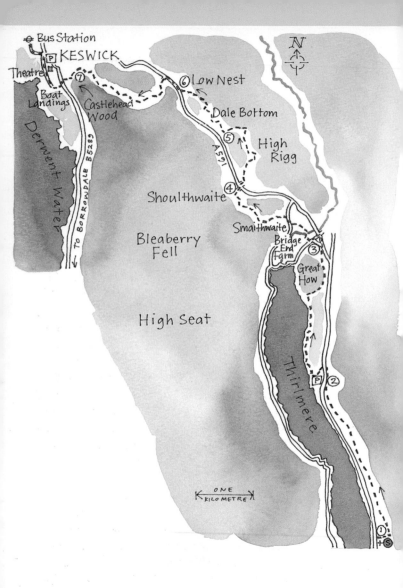

Bus Station
KESWICK
Theatre
Boat
Landings
Castlehead
Wood
⑦

⑥ Low Nest
Dale Bottom
⑤
High
Rigg
A591
④
Shoulthwaite
Smaithwaite
Bridge
End
Farm
③
Great
How
Derwent Water
TO BORROWDALE B5289
Bleaberry
Fell
High Seat
Thirlmere
P ②
N
ONE
KILOMETRE
P
①
Ⓢ

and Helm Crag. Go through a kissing gate and cross a bridge over a stream to reach a superb viewpoint: across the lake the long mountain wall includes Ullscarf, High Tove and High Seat. There is another footbridge as the route continues along a fairly narrow path, always clear and with occasional blue waymarks on rocks, trees and a post. By a signpost reading 'Thirlmere, Swirls, permissive path' join another forest roadway. Go ahead, gently uphill. There are gates before the path descends to a large car park, with public conveniences.

② Turn left to join the main A591 road. Turn right, by the roadside, and walk 150m to reach a popular parking area/viewpoint. Turn left and go down a few steps, and then left again, through a kissing gate, to follow a clear path signposted to 'The Dam, The Howe and Legburthwaite', descending to the shore of the lake; partway down is a stream with waterfalls/rapids. The path bears to the right, soon close to the lake shore, rising and falling. The King's Head Inn at Thirlspot comes into view as the track approaches the foot of Great How. At a signposted junction turn right towards 'Legburthwaite', descending along a good track; at the junction there is a clear view of Helvellyn. The track continues round the lower slopes of Great How, with How Beck below on the right.

③ Join the main road, the A591, and again walk by the roadside for 150m. Turn left along a minor road signposted 'public road round lake' to reach Bridge End Farm, with a small caravan site. Forty metres after the caravan site entrance turn right at a kissing gate signposted 'public footpath Smaithwaite ½ mile'. Follow the waymarked path to a gated bridge, a fine ancient structure, now rather decrepit. Turn left to continue, with a fence on the left; soon you will reach the long-disused Smaithwaite Farm, with a 1692 date. Ascend to join a minor road. Turn right, and then after 40m turn left and follow a broad unsurfaced roadway, with a comprehensive United Utilities signboard. Ignore a track on the right, and go through a waymarked kissing gate to continue along the roadway, close to the bottom edge of a wooded hillside. As the main track begins to ascend, with another comprehensive signboard, fork right, along a lesser track, and soon you will reach a kissing gate leading into Shoulthwaite Farm. Bear right to follow the farm access roadway to its junction with the A591.

④ Cross the A591 towards a long lay-by – a section of cut-off road. There is a short footpath with stiles at each end directly opposite the farm access road. Take this, and continue through a gate beside a stream, crossing a bridge. After another gate take a pleasant track that runs along the lower slopes of High Rigg, ascending gently. The track soon becomes a rough roadway as it approaches a house. At a junction turn left, go through a gate and follow the little road as far as the Dale Bottom caravan site.

⑤ Turn right at the main site entrance, almost opposite the reception/shop, and keep left of the caravans, along a site road with a wall close on the left. Go through a farm gate to a post with several waymarks and straight ahead, along a broad track. At another gate go left; the track, across a meadow, is well defined, with fine views of Skiddaw and Blencathra. Go through another gate and ascend along a grass track to a stile over a wall before joining the A591.

⑥ Cross and turn right, following the roadside footpath for about 400m uphill. Turn left through a kissing gate signposted to 'Walla Crag and Keswick'. There are more gates and a sharp right turn as the path turns to face Skiddaw. The route is clear, soon reaching a surfaced road. Turn left, and then after 20m right: descend to a waymarked little bridge, and continue through woodland with a rushing stream below on the right. There is a sudden view of Derwent Water and the fells beyond. The descent is steady. Go straight ahead at a junction with a sign saying 'public footpath Keswick'. Go left, downhill, at the next junction, with the stream still to the right. Pass Spring Farm to reach tarmac and the fringe of Keswick. Walk along a quiet little residential road as far as a footpath signposted to 'Castlehead and Lake Road'.

⑦ Turn left here and head for the wooded knoll, Castlehead. After a kissing gate, follow the clear track rising through the woodland, avoiding the left fork leading to the summit and soon descending to the Borrowdale road. Turn left along the track on the far side of the road for about 100m. Then turn right along a footpath signposted 'To the lake'; there are a few steps. The little path leads to Cockshot Wood. Turn right along the edge of the wood, taking a right fork directly into the huge car park adjacent to the Theatre by the Lake. Go through the car park and follow the access road, with its adjacent gardens and recreational facilities, as far as a road junction. Turn left and walk by the roadside for a little less than a kilometre to the bus station, by the side of Booth's supermarket.

Coleridge and Southey and their respective families lived for many years at Greta Hall, Keswick. Sometimes alone, sometimes accompanied by Dorothy and/or Mary, Wordsworth often walked from his home at Grasmere to visit these friends, a distance of about 21km (13 miles). After crossing Dunmail Raise, his route along the side of Thirlmere — in pre-reservoir days two lakes known as Wythburn Water and Leathes Water — would have been along the then main road, a cart road on the same side as the present A591, but lower down, now beneath the water, obviously more direct and with less rise and fall than the present route. He would have passed the Cherry Tree Inn at Wythburn, situated below the church, which was sited on higher ground. Part way along this road was the Rock of Names or Sara's Rock (see walk 10), where the Wordsworths from Grasmere met Coleridge from Keswick.

Greta Hall, Keswick

Dorothy records in her journal several such journeys. For instance, on 15 October 1800, there was an after-dinner walk: 'I walked with him to Wytheburn, and he went on to Keswick.' On 28 December 1801: 'William, Mary and I set off on foot to Keswick . . . We parted from William upon the Rays [Raise]. He joined us opposite Sara's Rock. He was busy in composition, and sate down upon the wall . . . Wm discovered that he had lost his gloves. He turned back but they were gone. We were tired and had bad headaches. We rested often. Once he left his Spenser [a garment], and Mary turned back for it, and found it upon the bank, where we had last rested. We reached Greta Hall at about ½ past 5 o'clock.' (The preoccupied poet being looked after by his female retinue?) And on 10 November: 'We left Keswick at 2 o'clock and did not arrive at G. [Grasmere] till 9 o'clock.'

The route to and from Keswick was occasionally varied, one visit being by way of St John's in the Vale and Threlkeld and others via Watendlath, crossing the high ground between Thirlmere and that village, a more arduous walk. As mentioned in walk 10, Wordsworth also recommended the road on the west side of the lake for its superior views of lake and mountains.

12. KESWICK

A pleasant circuit based on Keswick and the lovely valley of the River Greta, combining a length of the track bed of the former Penrith to Keswick railway line with a permissive footpath through Brundholme Woods. The route is never far from the river, which the outward section crosses no fewer than four times. Underfoot, the railway track bed is excellent, while the return footpath is generally good but with a long flight of steps and a steep valley side above the river that needs care.

Keswick has long been regarded as a fine little town, beautifully situated and full of interest for the visitor, including the museum and gallery on Station Road. The railway line from Penrith, where it connected with what is now the West Coast main line, to Keswick, Cockermouth and Workington was opened in 1864, bringing the prospect of considerable industrial traffic and the opening-up of the northern part of the Lake District to tourism. In the event, the industrial use declined at a relatively early stage, but tourism flourished until the inevitable rise in road usage after the Second World War. Despite great efforts to keep the line open, the Penrith to Keswick section finally closed to all traffic in 1972, the Keswick to Workington section having closed six years previously. For several miles to the east of Keswick station, the line now provides an official walking and cycling route, in the ownership of the National Park Authority. The authority also owns Keswick station, which has been sufficiently preserved to give some indication of its former glory.

You can add a circuit of Fitz Park, either before or after the main walk, for a — not very clear — view of the back of Greta Hall, adding 1.25km (¾ mile) to the length of the walk. Go through a gate and down a few steps close to the river to follow the made path with the river close on the left. Pass the end of a footbridge to reach a junction. Across the river, high on the far bank, is the rear of Greta Hall, largely obscured by trees. Turn right at the junction, and then right again to pass behind the sports pavilion, and rejoin Station Road.

DISTANCE	7km (4¼ miles)
ASCENT	130m (427ft)
START/PARKING	Roadside spaces along Station Road, by the Keswick Museum, controlled by disc, two hours allowed, grid reference 269238. Alternatively there are uncontrolled roadside spaces in the adjacent Brundholme Road.
REFRESHMENTS	None en route; wide choice in Keswick.
MAP	Ordnance Survey Explorer OL4, The English Lakes, north-western area, 1:25,000.

THE WALK

(S) Walk along Station Road, away from the town. Turn left at the Keswick Pool and Fitness Centre, passing to the right of the building.

(1) At a 'Keswick Railway Footpath' sign turn right, passing Keswick station, where there are public conveniences, and continue along the track bed of the former railway line, soon on an embankment. Cross the River Greta for the first time; Latrigg is prominent to the left, above a large council housing estate. Go under a road, passing the Brigham area, formerly an industrial centre, before ascending towards the main A66 road. Go under the A66. In this area the former railway alignment has been much altered; there is an extensive boardwalk high above the river. Next is Low Briery Holiday Village, where the platform of a former railway halt now provides access for the disabled. There is also the site of a former bobbin mill (see the display board). Cross the river again; the bowstring girder bridge, in this case with under arches, is characteristic of this line. Cross the river yet again. At the fourth river crossing the bowstring bridge has more conventional over arches.

(2) Go through a gate and turn left at once to descend a few steps to a stile, where there is a 'Keswick via Brundholme Woods, by kind permission of landowner' sign. Take the narrow path rising up the valley side. Go over a stile and continue along the delightful woodland path, which rises and falls above the river. Ignore any paths to the right. Ascend a long flight of shallow steps, keeping left at the top. There are occasional waymarks and a bridge over a stream before the path passes above

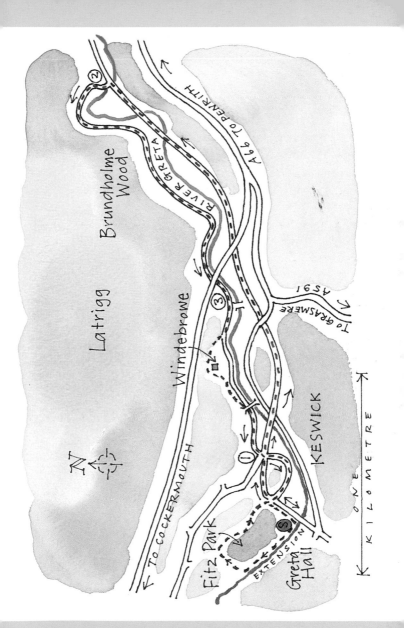

Calvert's bridge, near Keswick

the Low Briery complex. Go under the A66, pass a display board, and go through a kissing gate to join a road; to the left is a bridge across the river.

③ Turn right. The unsurfaced lane rises past a large white building before reaching Old Windebrowe (formerly Windy Brow), for many years occupied by the Calvert Trust, an outdoor activities organization. Join a minor road and turn left. Continue along the road for a short distance. At Brundholme Country Houses turn left; there is a 'footpath to Keswick' sign. After 50m turn right to take a signposted broad track descending gently through woodland. Cross a bridge before reaching a public road. Bear left along the side of the road, under a former railway bridge, and then behind the Keswick Hotel. This is Brundholme Road, leading to the parking area.

Keswick played an important part in the life of Wordsworth and his family. For many years his predecessor as Poet Laureate, Robert Southey, and his family lived at Greta Hall, a substantial house situated high on the bank on the south-west side of the River Greta. For some of those years the hall was also occupied by Samuel Coleridge, an even closer friend of the Wordsworths, and his family. William's walks between Grasmere and Keswick are well documented, as are the meetings with Coleridge by the side of Thirlmere (see walks 10 and 11). Uses of Greta Hall during the ensuing years have included a school boarding house. It is now a private residence, best seen from the top of the public car park on the town side of the Cumberland Pencil Museum and factory.

In 1793, before settling in the Lake District, Wordsworth had spent a month on the Isle of Wight with an old schoolfriend, William Calvert. In 1794, William and Dorothy stayed with Calvert at his home, Windy Brow (now Old Windebrowe), near Keswick. They made a seat in the grounds, for which both Wordsworth and Coleridge wrote inscriptions. Two months later Wordsworth returned to Windy Brow to look after Calvert's younger brother, Raisley, who was suffering from tuberculosis. Raisley died in 1795, leaving the then substantial amount of £900 to Wordsworth in his will; this was sufficient to free him from financial considerations and to allow him to pursue his life as a poet. Windy Brow remained a favourite place for the Wordsworths: in August 1800, for instance, Dorothy records walking in the woods with Coleridge and, a few days later, repairing the seat.

The River Greta was highly esteemed by Wordsworth. Late in life he wrote a sonnet 'To the River Greta', beginning:

Greta, what fearful listening when huge stones
Rumble along thy bed, block after block:
Or, whirling with reiterated shock,
Combat, while darkness aggravates the groans . . .

The old church at Great Crosthwaite, on the north-western fringe of Keswick, has a white marble monument to Robert Southey, with an epitaph by Wordsworth.

Latrigg, near Keswick

13. LODORE FALLS AND DERWENT WATER

A Keswick launch

This route follows the east shore of beautiful Derwent Water, starting at the Theatre by the Lake car park and visiting the celebrated Friar's Crag viewpoint on the way to the Lodore Falls. There is very little ascent and the path is easy to follow. After heavy rain, it is possible that some sections will be very wet, necessitating diversions along the adjacent Borrowdale road.

For the return to Keswick there is a choice: the Seatoller to Keswick bus service, stopping outside the Lodore Hotel, or, preferably, the Keswick launch, calling at the pier behind the Mary Mount Hotel.

DISTANCE	6.5km (4 miles)
ASCENT	35m (115ft)
START/PARKING	Large pay-and-display car park close to the Theatre by the Lake, Keswick, grid reference 266229.
REFRESHMENTS	Lodore Hotel, Theatre by the Lake, tea rooms at the Keswick boat landings, wide choice in Keswick.
MAP	Ordnance Survey Explorer OL4, The English Lakes, north-western area, 1:25,000.

THE WALK

Ⓢ Starting from the car park turn left, and pass the front of the theatre to reach the Keswick boat landings, where traditional launches operate a round-the-lake service and there are boats for hire. Continue along the lakeside roadway, with delightful views across the lake to Cat Bells. Pass a plaque in remembrance of Canon Rawnsley, the great Lake District conservation pioneer, and continue to the end of a little promontory, the deservedly popular Friar's Crag, facing the Borrowdale valley across the water.

① Retrace the route for a few metres and bear right to the John Ruskin memorial stone. Go down a few steps to join a more major track and turn right to a gate and a path along the shore of Strandshag Bay. The track continues along the edge of marshy woodland, over a footbridge and through a gate at the far end of the wood. Turn right here, passing Stable Hills, with Lord's Island close, and then Rampsholme Island, with St Herbert's Island more distant. You soon reach Calfclose Bay, with the National

Trust Millennium Stone, often part submerged. The track, with rough stony sections, and the Borrowdale road come close together.

② On reaching Ashness Gate jetty, used by the Keswick launches, continue along the shore of Barrow Bay and around a promontory.

③ At the Kettlewell car park (National Trust) cross the road to a signposted 'Footpath avoiding the road, towards Lodore'. Follow the path through woodland, for some distance close to the road, before it ascends gently towards the Lodore Falls, which you will have been hearing for some time.

④ At the splendid falls there are little paths which offer a choice of viewpoint. Return by going down the main path – which is initially rough – heading towards the back of the Lodore Hotel, passing a seat before crossing a footbridge over the torrent. Turn left to pass through the grounds of the hotel to the Borrowdale road. Turn right to reach the bus stop. Follow the road for a further 100m, following the signpost and forking left to reach the launch jetty.

Derwent Water and Cat Bells

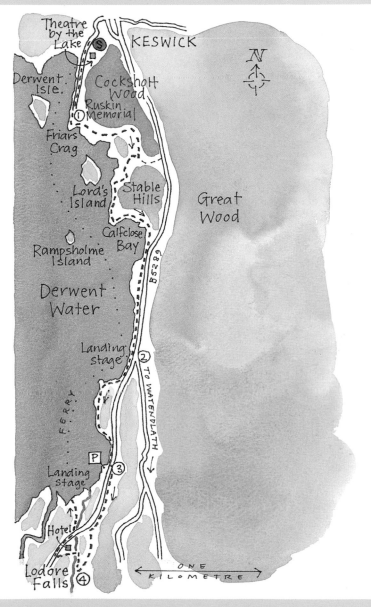

Theatre by the Lake

KESWICK

S

N

Derwent Isle

Cockshott Wood

Ruskin Memorial

①

Friars Crag

Lord's Island

Stable Hills

Great Wood

Calfclose Bay

Rampsholme Island

B5289

Derwent Water

Landing stage

②

TO WATENDLATH

FERRY

P

Landing Stage

③

Hotel

Lodore Falls

④

ONE KILOMETRE

LODORE FALLS AND DERWENT WATER   99

Wordsworth was obviously familiar with Derwent Water and Lodore from an early age. As this area was at the core of the part of the Lake District most extolled by the Picturesque Tourists, such as the poet Thomas Gray, Dr John Brown and William Gilpin, this is hardly surprising. In the poem 'An Evening Walk' — which he wrote at the age of eighteen while he was at Cambridge and was published five years later — he remembers:

His wizard course where hairy Derwent takes
Thro' crags, and forest glooms, and opening lakes,
Staying his silent waves, to hear the roar
That stuns the tremulous cliffs of High Lodore.

On their great tour of 1799, Wordsworth and Coleridge walked along the shore of Derwentwater. It seems likely that they would have expressed their disapproval of the excesses of Joseph Pocklington, a rich banker who had bought Vicar's Isle and other land in the area, including the site on which stands the Bowder Stone, and built extravagant and pseudo-historic structures, including a 'Druid's Temple', a 'hermitage' and a cascade to rival the nearby Lodore Falls. On 15 November the poets visited the falls, apparently making little comment.

Derwent Water and Cat Bells

14. THE DUDDON VALLEY

Even at times when Lakeland as a whole has large numbers of visitors, and Langdale and Borrowdale are overwhelmed, the Duddon valley remains an oasis of tranquillity. The upper part of the valley is rugged and desolate, with the road over the Wrynose Pass climbing high before its long descent into Little Langdale, but the middle Duddon is a rich mixture

The River Duddon

DISTANCE	8.75km (5½ miles)
ASCENT	183m (600ft)
START/PARKING	Forestry Commission Birks Bridge car park by the roadside 5km (3 miles) above Seathwaite, grid reference 236995.
REFRESHMENTS	Newfield Inn, Seathwaite or riverside picnic.
MAP	Ordnance Survey Explorer OL6, The English Lakes, south-western area, 1:25,000.

of bare rock, rushing waters and dense forest. High above, the shapely peak of Harter Fell faces the less distinctive side of the Coniston fells across the valley. The Forestry Commission has planted huge areas of the flanks of Harter Fell, not quite with the sensitivity that would now be required, but the middle Duddon as a whole remains highly attractive.

Despite its modest length, this walk is no easy ramble. The overall ascent is not great, but the riverside path is hard going: exposed rocks, tree roots and extensive mud all combine to impede progress. The reward for all this effort is close intimacy with a most beautiful stretch of this great river, with its green, tumbling waters. The return part of the route is altogether different, passing through the farming country of the valley of the Tarn Beck before crossing Troutal Tongue on a good path.

The suggested extension to the route (see point 2) visits Seathwaite, the main hamlet of the middle Duddon, with its church and inn, adding 1.5km (1 mile) to the length of the walk, plus a little in ascent.

THE WALK

(S) Start from the car park cross the utilitarian bridge over the river and immediately turn left to take a rather vague and muddy path running close to the forest boundary fence. There are marker posts along the way. The path passes the remains of a large stone gate pillar, rising a little on firmer ground.

(1) After less than 50m turn left along a better path leading to Birks Bridge, which spans a renowned rocky gorge. Do not cross; continue along the riverside path, which soon goes uphill to the right, with white waymarks, to reach the top of a rocky knoll. Take care with the rather vague path descending from the knoll as it heads for Seathwaite. There is a comparatively easy section through woodland set back from the river; otherwise the path stays close to the waterside, twisting and turning through the difficult terrain. Cross Wet Gill, with its pretty waterfall, before reaching a set of stepping stones, one of several that cross the Duddon. This set has a cable handhold but can be impassable when the river is high.

(2) Cross the river on the stepping stones and take the footpath slanting uphill to the right, through the bracken, to the valley road. Turn right and follow the road downhill to the bridge over Tarn Beck. (For the extended walk do not cross the stepping stones. Continue along the riverside path for a further 1.5km (1 mile); the

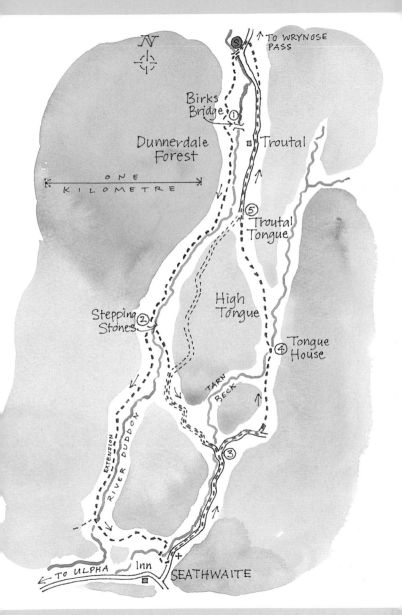

N

TO WRYNOSE
PASS

Birks
Bridge ①

Dunnerdale
Forest

Troutal

ONE
KILOMETRE

⑤ Troutal
Tongue

High
Tongue

Stepping ②
Stones

④ Tongue
House

TARN
BECK

EXTENSION

RIVER DUDDON

③

TO ULPHA   Inn   SEATHWAITE

Seathwaite

path includes an ascent to the right to pass
behind another knoll and a section across the
foot of a scree slope. Reaching a stone bridge,
with a 1934 construction plaque, cross the river
and follow the clear path towards Seathwaite,
crossing another bridge, over Tarn Beck, on the
way. Join the valley road opposite the church –
the Newfield Inn is a short diversion to the right.
To continue the circuit, turn left and walk by the
roadside to rejoin the basic route at point 3.)

③ Beyond the bridge turn sharp left at a
road junction and take the road signposted to
Coniston (unfit for motors). This is the start of
the famous Walna Scar route. Turn left at the first

junction, pass Hollin House and continue along a lane towards Tongue House. This area provides some of the best farming country of the middle Duddon, in complete contrast to the earlier part of the walk.

④ Fifty metres before reaching Tongue House, turn left to cross Tarn Beck on a waymarked footbridge, pass in front of Thrang Cottage and follow a little path to the left climbing quite steeply through woodland. You emerge at the open top of Troutal Tongue, with exposed rocks, bracken and good views, particularly of Harter Fell. The track descends to a stile before reaching the valley road at a 'public footpath' signpost.

⑤ Turn right and walk by the side of the quiet road, passing Troutal Farm. As the road bends to the left, take a signposted footpath, through a farm gate, ahead. The route is along the edge of boggy ground, heading for a stile over the wall ahead. Follow the clear track that traverses the pine plantation, rejoining the road about 100m beyond the entrance to the car park. Turn left to return.

Wordsworth's first acquaintance with the Duddon was as a schoolboy, when he walked over from Hawkshead with an adult friend to fish in the river, without success — 'the rain pouring torrents and worn out with fatigue'. Despite this unhappy experience, it is obvious that Wordsworth loved the Duddon valley. During long vacations from Cambridge he stayed with cousins at Broughton-in-Furness, spending many days exploring the valley. He made later visits in 1794 and with Mary in 1811.

In his *Guide to the Lakes* he comments: 'The water is perfectly pellucid, through which in many places are seen, to a great depth, their beds of rock, or of blue gravel, which give to the water itself an exquisitely cerulean colour: this is particularly striking in the rivers Derwent and Duddon, which may be compared, such and so various are their beauties, to any two rivers of equal length of course in any country.'

The Duddon is the only place in the whole of the Lake District that he singled out by name in the dedication of a set of poems, the Duddon Sonnets of 1818–20, published with considerable success in the latter year. In verse that, like the 'Duddon, long loved Duddon', flows 'pure, vigorous, free, and bright', the thirty-four sonnets broadly follow the course of the river, from its source high up Wrynose to the broad sands of the estuary — including Seathwaite and its celebrated parson, 'Wonderful Walker', 'Whose good works formed an endless retinue'. In the sonnets he displays his deep emotional response to the landscape and the reflections on the human condition it inspires. In the ninth sonnet, for instance, stepping stones prompt a reflection on youth and age —

> The struggling rill insensibly is grown
> Into a brook of loud and stately march,
> Crossed over and anon by plank and arch;
> And, for like use, lo! What might seem a zone
> Chosen for ornament: stone matched with stone
> In studied symmetry, with interspace

For the clear waters to pursue their race
Without restraint. — How swiftly have they flown,
Succeeding — still succeeding! Here the child
Puts, when the high-swoln flood runs fierce and wild,
His budding courage to the proof: — and here
Declining manhood learns to note the sly
And sure encroachments of infirmity,
Thinking how fast time runs, life's end how near!

— while in the final sonnet he contrasts the permanence of the
river with the mortality of man:

I thought of thee, my partner and my guide,
As being past away. Vain sympathies!
For, backward, Duddon! As I cast my eyes,
I see what was, and is, and will abide;
Still glides the stream, and shall not cease to glide;
The form remains, the function never dies;
While we, the brave, the mighty, and the wise,
We men, who in our morn of youth defied
The elements, must vanish; — be it so!

15. LOWESWATER

Although outdone in popularity by its bigger neighbours, Buttermere and Crummock Water, Loweswater is a charming lake with contrasting vistas, lending itself admirably to circumnavigation. To the north-west, beyond the head of the lake, is low hill country, very much the edge of the Lake District; to the south-east the lake shares the grandeur of the mountain panorama enjoyed by Buttermere and Crummock Water. From Loweswater, Melbreak may be seen at its best, an impressive end-on view that rather flatters this otherwise modest mountain. To the east the peaks of Whiteside and Grasmoor are dominant.

This gentle circuit provides a well-varied mixture of typical Lakeland walking.

DISTANCE	6.25km (4 miles)
ASCENT	70m (231ft)
START/PARKING	Choice of two informal roadside parking areas on the road beside the lake, grid reference 121224.
REFRESHMENTS	The well-signposted Kirkstile Inn is approximately 0.75km (½ mile) from the south-eastern end of this route; excellent lakeside picnic opportunities.
MAP	Ordnance Survey Explorer OL4, The English Lakes, north-western area, 1:25,000.

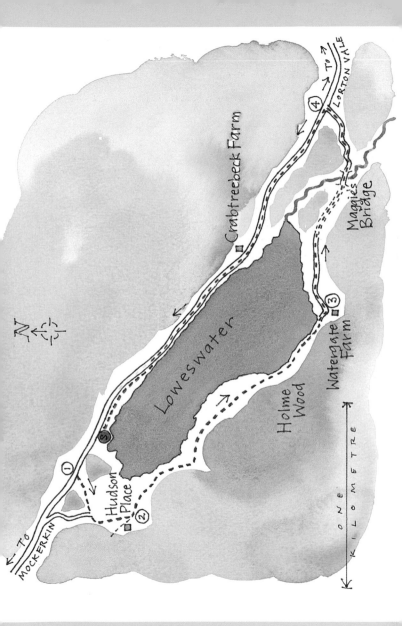

Crabtreebeck Farm

Loweswater

Holme Wood

Watergate Farm

Maggies Bridge

TO LORTON VALE

Hudson Place

TO MOCKERKIN

① ② ③ ④ ⑤

N

ONE KILOMETRE

THE WALK

One of the authors at Loweswater

(S) Starting from the first parking area walk along the roadside, north-west, towards Mockerkin.

(1) At the far end of the second parking area turn left; there is a 'public footpath Holme Wood ½ mile' sign. Go through a kissing gate and follow a path beside a tiny stream. Go over a stile and continue to a footbridge across Dub Beck. Go over the footbridge. Cross the mire by the head of the lake; the path is largely on boardwalks. Go through/over a gate/stile to join a surfaced access roadway. Turn left and ascend steadily towards Hudson Place, a large farmstead that includes a house with the date 1741 over the door.

(2) Go through gates, bearing left by a 'footpath' sign, to take a bramble-lined track descending towards the lake, with the great hump of Grasmoor in view ahead. After a

delightful open section, enter the National Trust Holme Wood at a gate. The track forks; either route will do, as they come together again by Holme Bothy, towards the far end of the wood. The woodland is very pleasant: a good mixture of trees, with some very old beech and other species close to the lake shore. The shapely hill above, right, is Carling Knott, 544m (1,785ft).

③ Leave the wood, pass the National Trust-owned Watergate Farm and turn left to follow the farm access road, crossing Maggie's Bridge over Dub Beck before reaching a small car parking area. Bear left, gently uphill, along the access road.

④ Join the Mockerkin road and turn left towards the parking area. Return along the roadside; 150m beyond Crabtreebeck Farm there is the start of a narrow, stony footpath along the lake shore that provides an attractive alternative to the roadside. After briefly rejoining the road, the path continues directly to the parking area.

Boat on Loweswater

When William toured the Lake District with Coleridge in 1799, they visited the area, Coleridge becoming increasingly excited as first Loweswater, then Crummock, and finally Buttermere came into view. William was very taken with Loweswater, writing in an early edition of his *Guide to the Lakes*:

> I am not sure that the circuit of this lake can be made on horseback; but every path and field in the neighbourhood would well repay the active exertions of the Pedestrian. Nor will the most hasty Visitant fail to notice with pleasure, that community of attractive and substantial houses which are dispersed over the fertile inclosures at the foot of those rugged Mountains, and form a most impressive contrast with the humble and rude dwellings which are usually found at the head of these far-winding Dales.

He also advises: 'Loweswater — This small lake is only approached to advantage from the other end; therefore any Traveller going by this road to Wasdale, must look back upon it.'

Gavel Fell, Loweswater

Carling Knott, Loweswater

16. BROTHERS WATER AND HARTSOP

An easy ramble, almost entirely level, on good tracks throughout. Brothers Water is a beautifully situated tarn, with several little shingle beaches that make good picnic sites. The road from Patterdale to Windermere passes the tarn before commencing the long ascent to the high and lonely Kirkstone Inn.

Hartsop Hall is one of Lakeland's oldest farms, with characteristic structural features.

Hartsop is one of the most attractive hamlets in the Lake District, sitting at the foot of Hartsop Dodd, with traditionally built old houses that display features such as spinning galleries and outside stairways.

DISTANCE	8km (5 miles)
ASCENT	50m (164ft)
START/PARKING	Car park at Cow Bridge by the side of the A592, 300m (328 yards) north-west of the junction with the Hartsop road, grid reference 403133.
REFRESHMENTS	Brotherswater Inn, Barn End bar, picnic sites by the side of Brothers Water.
MAP	Ordnance Survey Explorer OL5, The English Lakes, north-eastern area, 1:25,000.

FOLLOWING PAGES Hartsop Hall farm

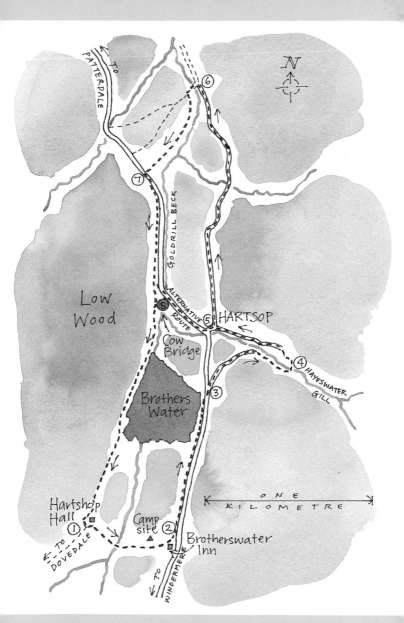

N

Low
Wood

GOLDRILL BECK

ALTERNATIVE ROUTE

HARTSOP

Cow
Bridge

Brothers
Water

HAYESWATER GILL

④

⑤

③

⑥

⑦

Ⓢ

TO PATTERDALE

ONE KILOMETRE

Hartsop
Hall

Camp
site

①

②

Brotherswater
Inn

TO DOVEDALE

TO WINDERMERE

THE WALK

🅢 Leave the parking area through a signposted little gate, close to a seat dated 1897 (VR). By the gate is a National Trust information board. Follow the broad, easy track by the side of tree-lined Goldrill Beck, which soon rises gently beside Brothers Water with views across to Hartsop hamlet. Ahead are the impressive Hartsop Dodd and Dove Crag, with the cleft of the Kirkstone Pass to their left.

Dove Crag

① When you reach the back of Hartsop Hall, turn left and continue along the hall's access road. (Before turning it is worth continuing a little further ahead for the splendid views up Dovedale.) Cross Kirkstone Beck on a wooden bridge and pass through a camping site; then pass the Barn End bar before ascending quite steeply towards the A592 road. At a junction keep left; the Brotherswater Inn is to the right.

② Immediately before the junction with the main road, fork left along a narrow but adequate path staying close to the roadside wall. Cross a tiny stream and then join the roadside very briefly before descending, now through woodland, close to the shore of Brothers Water. Leave the woodland at a kissing gate and then go up to another kissing gate to join the main road.

③ Cross the road, bearing slightly left to take a path rising up the bank on the far side. Bear left through a gate and continue along a good path, rising gently past wild briar. There are excellent traditional buildings by the wayside, including Fell Yeat. Continue along a broad track, ignoring a footbridge to the left. Go through a gate, after which the path rises gently. Among the grass beside the track orchids are profuse. Go through a gate and bear left to cross a bridge over Hayeswater Gill.

Bracket fungi, Hartsop Hall farm

④ Bear left again through a kissing gate to cross an informal car park and reach tarmac. Follow the road as it descends between the cottages of Hartsop towards the main road. (For an alternative shorter route back to the starting point, see page 117.)

⑤ Fifty metres before the junction with the main road turn right, along a tarmac-surfaced lane, signposted to Hartsop Fold. Pass Crossgates Farm, with its large, unsightly outbuildings. As the roadway bends right into Hartsop Fold, go straight ahead, where the lane, now unsurfaced, passes between stone walls. The wooden lodges of Hartsop Fold are relatively unobtrusive. The lane ends at a gate. Go through and cross Angletarn Beck, with its attractive waterfall and rapids, on a footbridge. Follow the path as it continues, with a little beck on the left and views towards Patterdale and of the Fairfield group of mountains across the valley. Keep left at a fork, descending through a gate to a junction.

⑥ Turn very sharp left, following the signpost reading 'public bridleway, Deepdale Bridge'. Cross Goldrill Beck on a farm bridge and immediately go over a stile on the left to follow an indistinct grass path by the side of the beck, along the top of the flood embankment. There are more stiles and some light woodland before you reach the main road, the A592.

⑦ Go across the road to a kissing gate opposite and bear left along a path which stays fairly close to the side of the road as it weaves its way delightfully through woodland before leading directly into the car park.

Wordsworth frequently walked through this area on his way to and from the house of his friends the Clarksons, at Eusemere near Pooley Bridge. According to Dorothy, during a return journey to Grasmere on 16 April 1802, she left William sitting on the bridge at the foot of Brothers Water (Cow Bridge) while she continued along the path on the right side of the lake, through woodland. The water under the boughs of the trees, the simplicity of the mountains and the exquisite beauty of the path captivated her: she hung over a gate and thought she could have stayed there for ever. On her return she found that William was writing a poem describing the sights and sounds that they had seen and heard. By the time that they reached the foot of the Kirkstone Pass, where they ate dinner before commencing the ascent, he had finished the poem:

> The Cock is crowing,
> The stream is flowing,
> The small birds twitter,
> The lake doth glitter,
> The green field sleeps in the sun;
> The oldest and youngest
> Are at work with the strongest;
> The cattle are grazing,
> Their heads never raising;
> There are forty feeding like one!
>
> Like an army defeated
> The snow hath retreated,
> And now doth fare ill
> On the top of the bare hill;
> The ploughboy is whooping-anon-anon.
> There's joy in the mountains;
> There's life in the fountains;
> Small clouds are sailing,
> Blue sky prevailing;
> The rain is over and gone!

In his *Guide to the Lakes* Wordsworth comments that the decaying hamlet of Hartsop is remarkable for its cottage architecture, also mentioning the 'lowly Hall of Hartshope [Hartsop] with its long roof and ancient chimneys'. He advises tourists to walk along the west side of Brothers Water and then to continue past Hartsop Hall to the point where a stream issues from a cove richly decorated with native wood (Dovedale). He believed that travellers never explored this spot but that those following his advice and looking back on the gleaming surface of Brothers Water, or forward to the precipitous sides and lofty ridges of Dove Crag, would be equally pleased with the beauty, the grandeur and the wildness of the scenery. He mentions that the name of the lake in old maps is 'Broaderwater', with the change to Brothers Water resulting from the tragic drowning of two brothers who had fallen through the ice about twenty years before.

Cottage at Hartsop

17. AIRA FORCE

One of the finest waterfalls in the country, Aira Force has long been a popular destination for a Lakeland excursion. Its accessibility has been enhanced by the National Trust, providers of a substantial car park and improvers of the footpaths leading to the main fall, which is spectacular after heavy or prolonged rainfall.

In addition to the main fall, the route set out below visits High Force, also very attractive, using paths that are rougher and steeper to make a pleasant circuit. Some sections will be muddy in wet weather but there are no other difficulties.

DISTANCE	3.25km (2 miles)
ASCENT	150m (492ft)
START/PARKING	National Trust car park with public conveniences, entered direct from A592, approximately 5km (3 miles) north-east of Glenridding, grid reference 400201.
REFRESHMENTS	Café at the car park, choice in Glenridding.
MAP	Ordnance Survey Explorer OL5, The English Lakes, north-eastern area, 1:25,000.

THE WALK

Ⓢ Leave the car park through a stone gateway at the top end, passing information boards and an 'Aira Force Waterfall ½ mile' notice. Take the broad track that leads up the valley to a gate and a National Trust 'Aira Force'

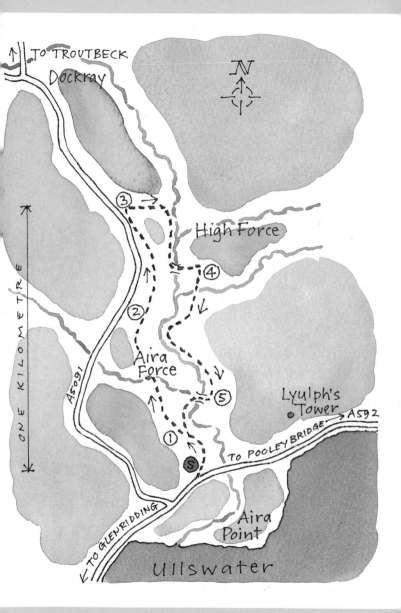

TO TROUTBECK

Dockray

N

③

High Force

④

②

Aira
Force

⑤

Lyulph's
Tower

A592

A5091

①

TO POOLEY BRIDGE

Ⓢ

ONE KILOMETRE

TO GLENRIDDING

Aira
Point

Ullswater

sign, ascending gently with the stream, Aira Beck,
below to the right. Pass another gate and enter woodland,
where the track is still broad and easy. Cross a bridge
over a small tributary stream to reach a junction within
a few metres.

① Bear left, uphill, go up rough steps and reach another
junction. Go left, through a little gate, and continue the
ascent. There are views of Ullswater and the mountains
beyond, including Place Fell and the Fairfield group.
The track is now a much narrower footpath.

High Force, Ullswater

② At another fork after 60m do not enter the woodland: turn right to a gate/stile. Go through/over this and continue along a grass path ascending gently through bracken, high above the stream. There is mud and parts of the path are not too distinct.

③ At a T-junction 80m before a wall turn right, along a more used path descending towards the stream. Go through a gate to reach the side of the stream, with turbulent rapids, a little way above High Force. Turn right to begin the descent on a clear but rough path beside the stream, soon reaching a viewpoint for High Force. The path continues along the top edge of woodland, with a wall on the right, along a glen apparently filled with rushing water – rapids and small falls. Cross the stream on a bridge over a deep gorge, and then turn right, up a rocky stairway. Bear right at the top.

④ After about 200m fork right, steeply downhill on a part-improved path. Soon you will reach the side of the stream; continue to a junction of paths, with a nicely arched stone bridge on the right, above the top of Aira Force. Do not cross the bridge. As the path forks, take the lower route, going down many steps. At the bottom of the steps a turn to the right leads to another stone bridge and the viewpoint for the main fall of Aira Force. After viewing, return to the main path, turning right to continue the descent. The path is soon much improved and there are a few steps down to an area with seat.

⑤ Cross a wooden footbridge, go up steps on the far side and rejoin the outward route at point 1. Turn left to return to the car park.

Wordsworth was a frequent visitor to the Ullswater area, often on his way to and from Eusemere, the home of his friends the Clarksons. The highly 'picturesque' scenery of the valley of the Aira Beck and its spectacular falls inspired him in the writing of three poems. Best known is 'The Somnambulist', an ancient tale of knightly love and death, which opens:

> List, ye who pass by Lyulph's Tower
> At eve; how softly then
> Doth Aira-force, that torrent hoarse,
> Speak from the woody glen!
> Fit music for a solemn vale!
> And holier seems the ground
> To him who catches on the gale
> The spirit of a mournful tale,
> Embodied in the sound.

Lyulph's Tower, an ancient hunting lodge, can still be seen, through the trees, from the car park.

In 'The Waterfall and the Eglantine' the roar of the water curtails the overheard discussion between the waterfall and the 'poor briar rose' who it believes is blocking its way.

> What more he said I cannot tell,
> The Torrent down the rocky dell
> Came thundering loud and fast;
> I listened, nor aught else could hear;
> The Briar quaked — and much I fear
> Those accents were his last.

Aira Force, Ullswater

18. MARTINDALE

Martindale is a sizeable valley tucked away to the south-east of Ullswater, entirely devoted to farming. As road access is limited to a minor cul-de-sac from Pooley Bridge, the dale remains entirely quiet and peaceful, at least above the parish church, where space for car parking does encourage a few visitors. There is a protected herd of red deer.

This linear walk makes use of the attractive 'steamer' service on Ullswater to reach the starting place at Howtown. Much of the route is along the Martindale road, which most walkers will find perfectly acceptable. The ascent of the broad ridge of Beda Fell is long and steady, on a narrow but clear path. The descent to Patterdale is rough underfoot.

In addition to the present parish church of St Peter, Martindale, the route passes the former church, now standing lonely further up the valley.

DISTANCE	11.25km (7 miles)
ASCENT	410m (1,346ft)
START/PARKING	Car park, with public conveniences near by, by the steamer pier at Glenridding, grid reference 390170.
REFRESHMENTS	At the steamer pier and the nearby boating centre.
MAP	Ordnance Survey Explorer OL5, The English Lakes, north-eastern area, 1:25,000.

Boredale Hause

THE WALK

(S) From the boat landing at Howtown, follow the signpost 'to road, Howtown'. You soon pass through a gate to join the road. Turn right, cross a bridge over Fusedale Beck, pass the entrance to the Howtown Hotel and continue along the road. Ahead, right is Hallin Fell. As the road rises steeply, there are grass paths that cut out some of the sharp bends. From the top of the road the great bulk of Place Fell comes into view ahead. Pass car-parking areas and reach the parish church of St Peter, Martindale, a short diversion to the left.

(1) Continue along the road, downhill, passing a cottage and the junctions with the road from Sandwick. Fork left and head into Martindale. As the road dips to the right, the old church of St Martin is on the left. Note the poster concerning the Red Deer Conservation Area. Cross Christy Bridge over Howe Grain Beck and pass Winter Crag, and then a ruinous farm (Thrang Crag). In front, Nab End is impressive at the division of the valley, Ramps Gill to the left and Bannerdale to the right. Pass between farm buildings before reaching Dale Head, the end of the road.

(2) At the entrance to the farm turn right at a 'Patterdale' sign, stride over a stream and go through a little gate to start the long ascent. Cross a plank bridge to recross the stream and continue to ascend above the farm. At a fork, keep right, close to a wall. The path is generally

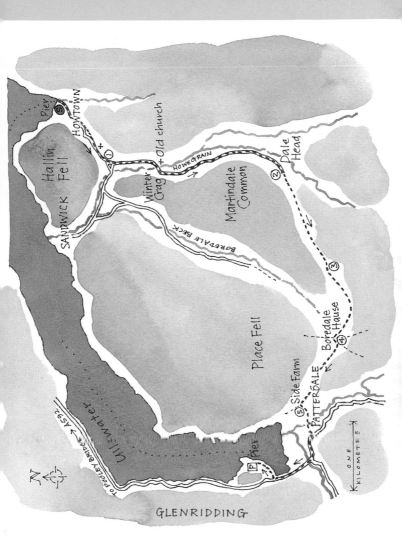

Pier

HOWTOWN

Old church

Hallin Fell

SANDWICK FELL

Winter Crag

HOWEGRAIN

Martindale Common

Dale Head

Boredale BECK

Place Fell

Boredale Hause

Side Farm

PATTERDALE

Pier

Ullswater

To POOLEY BRIDGE A592

N

GLENRIDDING

ONE KILOMETRE

narrow, often through bracken, but it is always clear as it rises inexorably across the hillside. The views are of the mountains surrounding the head of Bannerdale, northern outliers of the High Street range. Pass a gate/stile, and then the ruin of a tiny building; up to the right are the crags of Bedafell Knott. As you gain height, the higher parts of High Street come into view to the south.

③ There is a small cairn near the top and there are views towards St Sunday Crag, Helvellyn and Place Fell, with Patterdale below. The path now has boggy areas as it weaves its way across the hillside down towards Boredale Hause, visible ahead; Boredale is the deep valley to the right. The path crosses Freeze Beck, making a sharp little rise before resuming the descent towards Boredale Hause.

④ At an open area with a cairn, the meeting place of several routes just below the Hause, go ahead, towards Ullswater, on a path that terraces down the hillside, with superb views, including Brothers Water to the left, the Fairfield and Helvellyn ranges, Ullswater and Patterdale. At a fork keep left, steeply downhill, to reach a tarmac road, through a gate. Turn right, through another gate, and follow an unsurfaced road past a row of cottages, descending gently to Side Farm.

Old church, Martindale

(5) Turn left between the farm buildings, along the farm access roadway signposted 'Glenridding'. Cross Goldrill Beck and join the A592 by the side of the George Starkey hut. Turn right and walk by the road towards Glenridding, passing St Patrick's Church, using sections of path separated from the road where possible. At the far end of a section terraced above the road, cross over to a gate beside the boating centre, where refreshments are available. A path across a meadow leads directly to the car park.

On 28 December 1801, William, Mary and Dorothy set off from Grasmere to Keswick, reaching Greta Hall at 5.30 p.m. after mishaps such as William losing his gloves. The following day the Wordsworths headed for the Clarksons' house at Eusemere, near Pooley Bridge, where they spent the next few days, mainly walking in the area, including 'towards Martindale'.

On 9 November 1805 Wordsworth 'took a boat to row down the lake' (Ullswater). After commenting on the fish population of Ullswater, in his *Guide to the Lakes* Wordsworth writes that they pursued their way 'towards Martindale along a pleasant path', crossing 'the one-arched bridge, below the chapel, with its bare ring of mossy wall and single yew tree'. This is obviously the old church of St Martin, where the ancient yew is still *in situ*. He continues:

At the last house in the dale we were greeted by the master . . . He invited us to enter . . . The good woman treated us with oaten Cake, new and crisp; and after this welcome refreshment and rest, we proceeded on our return to Patterdale by a short cut over the mountains . . . Towards its head, this valley splits into two parts; and in one of these (that to the left) there is no house, nor any building to be seen but a cattle shed on the side of a hill . . . Near the entrance of the other division stands the house where we were entertained, and beyond the enclosures of that farm there are no other . . .

Our ascent even to the top was very easy; when it was accomplished we had exceedingly fine views . . . Looked down into Boardale . . . smooth and bare, a long, narrow, deep, cradle-shaped glen . . . After having walked some way along the top of the hill, came in view of Glenridding and the mountains at the head of Grisedale . . .

A rough and precipitous peat track brought us down to our friend's house.

Old church, Martindale

Chest, Martindale church

19. POOLEY BRIDGE AND ULLSWATER

A circuit over the high ground to the south-east of Ullswater, with the return to Pooley Bridge along the lake shore. The moorland of Moor Divock has a comprehensive late Neolithic/early Bronze Age ritual landscape, with field clearance cairns and features such as 'The Cockpit'. The much later Roman road High Street passes through this area. Pooley Bridge is a pleasant village, popular in high season, with the terminus of the Ullswater 'steamer' service.

    The moorland tracks are excellent underfoot, but some short lengths of farm path are a little overgrown, with several stiles. There is some mud in wet weather. The return route uses a section of the Howtown road, generally quiet. The majority of the ascent is in the initial climb from Pooley Bridge to Moor Divock, long and steady but not steep.

DISTANCE	11.5km (7¼ miles)
ASCENT	230m (755ft)
START/PARKING	Two pay-and-display car parks in Pooley Bridge, grid reference 470244; also some roadside spaces.
REFRESHMENTS	Inns and cafés in Pooley Bridge village.
MAP	Ordnance Survey Explorer OL5, The English Lakes, north-eastern area, 1:25,000.

THE WALK

S Walk from the bridge at Pooley Bridge along the village street, past toilets, tourist information, shops, inns and cafés. After St Paul's Church, fork right for 'Howtown and Martindale'. Pass the Parkin Memorial Hall.

① At a crossroads go straight across and take a cul-de-sac signposted to 'Hillcroft Camping Site'. Ascend steadily along the minor road, which soon has views over Ullswater. Roehead is to the left as you reach the end of the road. Go through a gate with a 'public bridleway, Helton' signpost and continue along a broad stony track, still ascending towards Moor Divock, with Heughscar Hill to the left.

② At a major cross paths with a substantial cairn, turn right. Soon you cross a stream. At the next junction turn right again. A few metres to the left is 'The Cockpit', a stone circle, the most remarkable of the many prehistoric features of the moor. Turn right and for a short distance you follow part of the famed Roman road called High Street. Stay with the clear track as it heads for the top edge of the woodland at Barton Park. Cross a valley with a rushing stream, Aik Beck, and ascend to the right to a signpost reading 'public bridleway, Howtown 2¾ miles'. There is a wall on the right as the track continues; the views now embrace a good deal of the spectacular head of Ullswater, including Helvellyn. Continue along a section beautifully terraced across the hillside below the crags that mark the edge of Barton Fell. Pass above Auterstone Wood, and then the farm of the same name. Cross Swarthbeck Gill on a bridge.

③ Turn sharp right through a gate on the right signposted 'public bridleway to the Howtown road'. Descend to Swarthbeck Farm. Opposite a barn turn right and cross the stream by a bridge, and continue through a gate and along a grass path at the lower edge of a field. Go through a waymarked gate, over a stile on the left and then, after 30m, over a waymarked stile on the right. The faint path stays close to the wall on the right before reaching a stile beside a gate. Go over this and pass through light woodland to join a farm access road. Turn right, passing in front of a terrace of cottages. After 50m turn left, over a stile, and follow a grass path, descending gently. After going down a steep grass bank and crossing a boggy stream, join the Howtown road at a gate.

④ Turn right to walk by the roadside for approximately 2km (1¼ miles), passing behind the Sharrow Bay Hotel and the Ullswater Yacht Club. There are views of the lake between the trees.

⑤ At Waterside House turn sharp left at a 'footpath, Pooley Bridge' sign. Pass between the buildings, towards the edge of the lake, bearing right at another signpost. Continue through the extensive camping site, keeping to the edge of the lake at any junction of tracks and heading towards the wooded Dunmallard Hill. Leave the camping site through a little gate; the track now goes along a shingle beach, one of

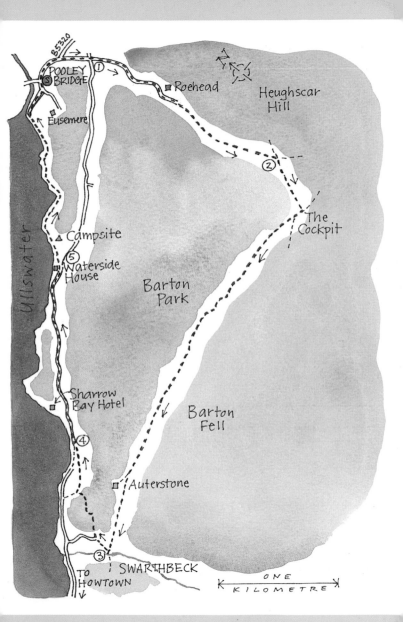

B5320

POOLEY
BRIDGE ⑤

① →

Eusemere

Roehead

Heughscar
Hill

②

Ullswater

△ Campsite

⑤

Waterside
House

Barton
Park

The
Cockpit

Barton
Fell

Sharrow
Bay Hotel

④

Auterstone

③ SWARTHBECK

TO
HOWTOWN

ONE
KILOMETRE

POOLEY BRIDGE AND ULLSWATER   143

the most attractive lakeside routes in the district. Cross
two footbridges and a boardwalk as the clear path heads
for Pooley Bridge. After a wooded section and almost
opposite the lake's steamer landing jetty, Eusemere is
up to the right, not easily seen from the path. Leave the
lake on a broad, rising track. Go through a gate to reach
a roadway; turn left to return to the bridge. For the main
National Park Authority car park, cross the road to a
little gate.

Daffodils by Ullswater

The area around Pooley Bridge was familiar territory to Wordsworth.

His great walking tour of the Lake District with Samuel Coleridge in 1799 terminated at Pooley Bridge. More significantly, just outside the village is Eusemere, the home of Thomas and Catherine Clarkson, the notable anti-slave trade campaigners with whom William and Dorothy had an enduring friendship. Dorothy records visits to Eusemere in her journal, the usual route from Grasmere being over the Kirkstone Pass to Patterdale and along the north-western shore of Ullswater. It was on returning from Eusemere on 15 April 1802 that she recorded:

When we were in the woods beyond Gowbarrow Park we saw a few daffodils close to the water-side. We fancied that the lake had floated the seeds ashore, and that the little colony had so sprung up. But as we went along there were more and yet more; and at last, under the boughs of the trees, we saw that there was a long belt of them along the shore, about the breadth of a country turnpike road. I never saw daffodils so beautiful. They grew among the mossy stones about and about them; some rested their heads upon these stones as on a pillow for weariness; and the rest tossed and reeled and danced, and seemed as if they verily laughed with the wind, that blew upon them over the lake; they looked so gay, ever glancing, ever changing. This wind blew directly over the lake to them. There was here and there a little knot, and a few stragglers a few yards higher up; but they were so few as not to disturb the simplicity, unity, and life of that one busy highway.

Two years later William converted Dorothy's account into:

I wandered lonely as a cloud
That floats on high o'er vales and hills,
When all at once I saw a crowd,
A host, of golden daffodils;
Beside the lake, beneath the trees,
Fluttering and dancing in the breeze.

Continuous as the stars that shine
And twinkle on the milky way,
They stretched in never ending line
Along the margin of a bay;
Ten thousand saw I at a glance,
Tossing their heads in sprightly dance.

The waves beside them danced; but they
Out-did the sparkling waves in glee;
A poet could not be but gay,
In such a jocund company;
I gazed — and gazed — but little thought
What wealth the show to me had brought;

For oft when on my couch I lie
In vacant or in pensive mood,
They flash upon that inward eye
Which is the bliss of solitude;
And then my heart with pleasure fills,
And dances with the daffodils.

9. COCKERMOUTH AND THE RIVER DERWENT

A circuit starting and finishing in the centre of Cockermouth, the route including the village of Papcastle, on the site of the Roman fort of Derventio. The walk continues along the line of the Roman road that connected Derventio with Alagna, at the north end of Maryport. For some distance the return stays close to the Broughton Beck and to the line of the long-defunct branch railway that connected Dearham with the

Wordsworth House, Cockermouth

Penrith to Workington line near Brigham. Following the path by the side of the River Derwent back to Papcastle and Cockermouth completes the circuit.

The footpaths are not difficult to follow, having ample waymarking, and they are mostly reasonable underfoot, although the section following Papcastle is likely to be wet at times. There are no serious ascents but numerous stiles.

Cockermouth is an attractive small town, well situated on the fringe of the Lake District at the confluence of the Rivers Derwent and Cocker, with plenty of shops, inns and other facilities.

DISTANCE	9.5km (6 miles)
ASCENT	90m (295ft)
START/PARKING	Choice of parking areas in Cockermouth. Wakefield Road pay-and-display car park is on the line of the walk, grid reference 117309. For simplicity the walk directions start at the statue of the Earl of Mayo, prominent in the middle of the main street.
REFRESHMENTS	Choice of inns and cafés in Cockermouth.
MAP	Ordnance Survey Explorer OL4, The English Lakes, north-western area, 1:25,000.

THE WALK

(S) Starting from the statue of the Earl of Mayo head west along the main street. Turn right at Bridge Street, after the library, where there is a 'memorial gardens' sign. (A little further along Main Street is Wordsworth House, with two small Wordsworth memorial sculptures across the road.) Cross the River Derwent on a long footbridge, and pass a children's play area and the Wakefield Road car park on the left; to the right is a factory building. Join a road for a short distance before bearing left at a 'footpath' sign and following a track between stone walls, close to Derwent Mills.

(1) Cross the main road, the A594, and continue along the minor road to Papcastle village. To the left is a former mill, now converted into flats. The road, with roadside footpath, rises past the chapel-like old pump house. There are views over the broad Derwent valley before you reach the centre of the village. Stay with the through road, ascending again before descending gently to cross a bridge over the Papcastle by-pass.

The River Derwent at Cockermouth

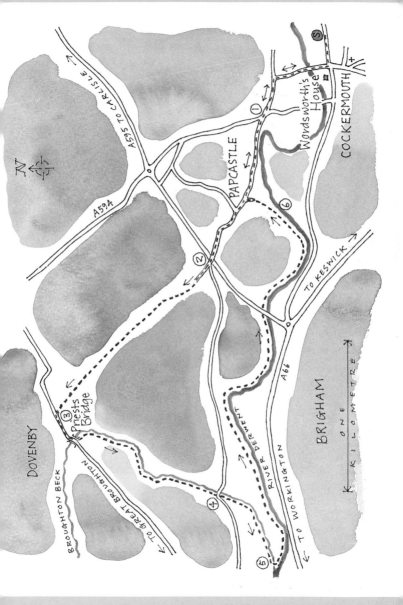

N

A595 TO CARLISLE

A594

PAPCASTLE

① ②

⑥

Wordsworth's House

COCKERMOUTH

+

TO KESWICK

A66

RIVER DERWENT

BRIGHAM

ONE KILOMETRE

DOVENBY

③ Priests Bridge

BROUGHTON BECK

TO GREAT BROUGHTON

④

⑤

TO WORKINGTON

COCKERMOUTH AND THE RIVER DERWENT   **151**

② Turn right immediately after the bridge, over a stile; there is a sign reading 'public footpath, Priests Bridge'. Go left, down a few steps, to continue. The path rises gently between banks, possibly wet underfoot. There are frequent stiles, mostly waymarked, as the path, faint in places, follows the edges of fields, on the alignment of the former Roman road, through open countryside. Aim for the left edge of a coniferous plantation. Go across the middle of a field to reach a signposted gate.

③ Join a minor road, turning left to walk down to Priests Bridge. Cross the bridge, over Broughton Beck, beside which ran the former branch railway line. A short distance upstream is a house that was formerly the private station serving nearby Dovenby Hall. Immediately over the bridge turn left and follow a footpath signposted to 'Broughton Bridge'. The attractive little path stays close to the beck, soon passing under the remains of a substantial railway bridge. Along the way there are stiles, with the former railway line evident on the far side of the beck. There is woodland and a few steps before the path passes a brick building on the right, with a former quarry behind. Join the quarry access roadway and bear left to reach a gate and a minor road.

④ Turn left for 20m (to the left is a house that was formerly Papcastle station). Turn right, over a stile in the wall, with a 'Broughton High Bridge' signpost. Continue, with the beck still on the left and the former railway line on the far side. Go over stiles, wooden steps and a boardwalk. Pass the end of a farm bridge, and you soon reach the confluence of the beck with the River Derwent. Cross a footbridge on the left.

The River Derwent behind Wordsworth House at Cockermouth

⑤ Head back towards Cockermouth along the broad Derwent valley, close to the side of the river. Pass the abutments of the bridge that carried the railway across the river. The path is never far from the water; with the exception of a short, steep rise and fall, it is level and easy to follow. There are bridges over two tributary streams. Pass under the Papcastle by-pass road and continue.

⑥ At a waymarked gate by the side of a single-storey building, bear left and ascend along a lane leading to Papcastle village. Rejoin the outward route, turning right to return to Cockermouth.

William Wordsworth was born in Cockermouth on 7 April 1770, the second child (after Richard, his elder brother) of John and Ann Wordsworth. John was a lawyer, working for Sir James Lowther, the wealthiest and most powerful landowner of the area, who owned the house in which the Wordsworth family lived. By all accounts William had a happy early childhood; during the four years after his birth the family was expanded by the birth of a sister, Dorothy, and two brothers, John and Christopher. Most importantly, the situation of the house, which backed on to the River Derwent and was within easy reach of the adjacent countryside, gave William the opportunity to develop an awareness and appreciation of the wonders of nature at a very early stage.

The idyllic childhood came to an end when his mother died in 1778. The boys stayed for a while with their father in Cockermouth, but Dorothy was sent to live with relatives in Halifax. In 1779 William and his brother Richard were sent away to school in Hawkshead (see walk 8).William always looked back fondly upon this early childhood. In his great autobiographical poem *The Prelude*, he wrote of the River Derwent:

Was it for this
That one, the fairest of all rivers, loved
To blend his murmurs with my Nurse's song,
And from his alder shades, and rocky falls,
And from his fords and shallows, sent a voice
That flowed along my dreams? For this didst thou
O Derwent, travelling over the green plains
Near my 'sweet birth place' didst thou beauteous Stream
Make ceaseless music through the night and day, . . .

Beloved Derwent! fairest of all Streams
Was it for this that I, a four year's child'
A naked Boy among thy silent pools
Made one long bathing of a summer's day?

Basked in the sun, or plunged into thy streams,
Alternate, all a summer's day, or coursed
Over the sandy fields, and dashed the flowers
Of yellow grunsel, or when crag and hill,
The woods and distant Skiddaw's lofty height
Were bronzed with a deep radiance, stood alone,
A naked Savage in the thunder shower?

The Wordsworth family house was a substantial and elegant late seventeenth-century building, close to the town centre. Improvements were made during the eighteenth century. After John Wordsworth's death in 1783, there is evidence that the property was neglected. William and Dorothy revisited in 1794, finding 'all . . . in ruin'. Passing the house again in 1828, Dorothy noted: 'Life has gone from my Father's Court.'

Later in the nineteenth century the house was renovated; for the early part of the twentieth century it was occupied by a medical practice. When, in 1937, it was proposed to sell the house to a bus company for demolition and redevelopment, the Wordsworth Memorial Fund was formed, purchasing the house for £1,625. The house was handed to the National Trust in 1938 and opened to the public in 1939, and it has since remained open, with both interior and garden restored to late eighteenth-century authenticity.

Across the road from the house is a small bust of Wordsworth.

FURTHER INFORMATION

There is an enormous amount of available literature concerning Wordsworth and his family. For the non-specialist reader, the following is a very short list of books and booklets which we have found to be most useful:

John Dawson and David Briggs, *Wordsworth's Duddon Revisited*, Cicerone, 1988

Collette Clark, *Home at Grasmere*, Penguin, 1960

Stephen Hebron, *William Wordsworth* (British Library Writers' Lives), British Library, 2000

Richard J. Hutchings (ed.), *The Wordsworth Poetical Guide to the Lakes: An Illustrated Anthology*, Rydal Mount and Gardens, 1977

Molly Lefebure, *The Illustrated Lakes Poets*, Tiger Books International, 1992

Grevel Lindop, *A Literary Guide to the Lake District*, Chatto & Windus, 1993

William Wordsworth, *Guide to the Lakes* (ed. Ernest de Selincourt), 5th edition, Oxford University Press, 1977

Dorothy Wordsworth, *Illustrated Lakeland Journals*, Diamond Books, 1991

Three Wordsworth homes are open to the public:

Wordsworth House (National Trust)
Main Street, Cockermouth, Cumbria CA13 9RX
Telephone: 01900 820884 (infoline)
www.nationaltrust.org.uk/main/w-wordsworthhouse

Dove Cottage, the Wordsworth Museum and Art Gallery (Wordsworth Trust)
Grasmere, Cumbria LA22 9SH
Telephone: 015394 35544
www.wordsworth.org.uk

Rydal Mount and Gardens (Wordsworth family)
Rydal, Near Ambleside, Cumbria LA22 9LU
Telephone: 015394 33002
www.rydalmount.co.uk

In each case illustrated booklets are available at
the property, together with a range of Wordsworth
publications.

ACKNOWLEDGMENTS

The authors would like to thank Peter Elkington and
John Hartley of Rydal Mount and Alex Black of the
Wordsworth Trust, Dove Cottage, for helpful advice
and encouragement.

INDEX

Page numbers in *italic* refer to photographs